THE
VIKINGS

Other titles in the *Lost Civilizations* series include:

LOST CIVILIZATIONS

THE VIKINGS

Allison Lassieur

LUCENT BOOKS
P.O. BOX 289011
SAN DIEGO, CA 92198-9011

Library of Congress Cataloging-in-Publication Data

Lassieur, Allison.
 The Vikings / by Allison Lassieur.
     p. cm. — (Lost civilizations)
Includes bibliographical references and index.
Summary: Discusses the history, culture, religion, arts and crafts, and voyages of the
Vikings.
 ISBN 1-56006-816-7
 1. Vikings—Juvenile literature. 2. Civilization, Viking—Juvenile literature. [1.
Vikings.] I. Title. II. Lost civilizations (San Diego, Calif.)
 DL65 .L375 2001
 948'.022—dc21

                                                              00-012491

Copyright © 2001 by Lucent Books, Inc.
P.O. Box 289011, San Diego, CA 92198-9011
Printed in the U.S.A.

CONTENTS

FOREWORD

"What marvel is this?" asked the noted eighteenth-century German poet and philosopher, Friedrich Schiller. "O earth . . . what is your lap sending forth? Is there life in the deeps as well? A race yet unknown hiding under the lava?" The "marvel" that excited Schiller was the discovery, in the early 1700s, of two entire ancient Roman cities buried beneath over sixty feet of hardened volcanic ash and lava near the modern city of Naples, on Italy's western coast. "Ancient Pompeii is found again!" Schiller joyfully exclaimed. "And the city of Hercules rises!"

People had known about the existence of long lost civilizations before Schiller's day, of course. Stonehenge, a circle of huge, very ancient stones had stood, silent and mysterious, on a plain in Britain as long as people could remember. And the ruins of temples and other structures erected by the ancient inhabitants of Egypt, Palestine, Greece, and Rome had for untold centuries sprawled in magnificent profusion throughout the Mediterranean world. But when, why, and how were these monuments built? And what were the exact histories and beliefs of the peoples who built them? A few scattered surviving ancient literary texts had provided some partial answers to some of these questions. But not until Pompeii and Herculaneum started to emerge from the ashes did the modern world begin to study and re-

construct lost civilizations in a systematic manner.

Even then, the process was at first slow and uncertain. Pompeii, a bustling, prosperous town of some twenty thousand inhabitants, and the smaller Herculaneum met their doom on August 24, A.D. 79 when the nearby volcano, Mt. Vesuvius, blew its top and literally erased them from the map. For nearly seventeen centuries, their contents, preserved in a massive cocoon of volcanic debris, rested undisturbed. Not until the early eighteenth century did people begin raising statues and other artifacts from the buried cities; and at first this was done in a haphazard, unscientific manner. The diggers, who were seeking art treasures to adorn their gardens and mansions, gave no thought to the historical value of the finds. The sad fact was that at the time no trained experts existed to dig up and study lost civilizations in a proper manner.

This unfortunate situation began to change in 1763. In that year, Johann J. Winckelmann, a German librarian fascinated by antiquities (the name then used for ancient artifacts), began to investigate Pompeii and Herculaneum. Although he made some mistakes and drew some wrong conclusions, Winckelmann laid the initial, crucial groundwork for a new science—archaeology (a term derived from two Greek words meaning "to talk about ancient things." His book, *History of the Art of Antiquity*, became a model for the first generation of archaeologists to follow in their efforts to understand other lost civilizations. "With unerring sensitivity," noted scholar C.W. Ceram explains, "Winckelmann groped toward original insights, and expressed them with such power of language that the cultured European world was carried away by a wave of enthusiasm for the antique ideal. This . . . was of prime importance in shaping the course of archaeology in the following century. It demonstrated means of understanding ancient cultures through their artifacts."

In the two centuries that followed, archaeologists, historians, and other scholars began to piece together the remains of lost civilizations around the world. The glory that was Greece, the grandeur that was Rome, the cradles of human civilization in Egypt's Nile valley and Mesopotamia's Tigris-Euphrates valley, the colorful royal court of ancient China's Han Dynasty, the mysterious stone cities of the Maya and Aztecs in Central America—all of these and many more were revealed in fascinating, often startling, if sometimes incomplete detail by the romantic adventure of archaeological research. This work, which continues, is vital. "Digs are in progress all over the world," says Ceram. "For we need to understand the past five thousand years in order to master the next hundred years."

Each volume in the *Lost Civilizations* series examines the history, works, everyday life, and importance of ancient cultures. The archaeological discoveries and methods used to gather this knowledge are stressed throughout. Where possible, quotes by the ancients themselves, and also by later historians, archaeologists, and other experts support and enliven the text. Primary and secondary sources are carefully documented by footnotes and each volume supplies the reader with an extensive Works Consulted list. These and other research tools, including glossaries and time lines, afford the reader a thorough understanding of how a civilization that was long lost has once more seen the light of day and begun to reveal its secrets to its captivated modern descendants.

A CULTURE ON THE MOVE

In England they were called Danes. The Germans called them Ashmen. The Irish knew them as Gaill (Foreigners) or Lochlannaigh (Northerners). Spanish Arabs called them Majus (Heathens). In the eastern areas of the world, they were known as the Rus. Today they are known simply as the Vikings.

The popular image of Vikings is one of wild blond warriors in full battle dress, spoiling for a fight. They built magnificent long ships that sliced through the water at great speeds; they killed, pillaged, and destroyed everything in their wake. They stole or destroyed precious Christian artifacts made of gold and silver. They kidnapped people and sold them into slavery for profit. To many, the Vikings represented all that was frightening about life in the Viking Age, which lasted from 793 to 1066.

While the popular image of Vikings today is that of bloodthirsty warriors, the Vikings were also masters of technology, international trade, and law.

This impression of the Vikings came mainly from the terrified and beaten Christian monks who witnessed Viking raids firsthand. The monks wrote of terror, blood, and death. In their eyes the Vikings were sent by a wrathful God as punishment for some wrongdoing. Documents and letters are filled with vivid descriptions of Vikings, and these descriptions have shaped the modern view of who the Vikings really were.

But the Viking civilization was much more than thievery and battle, raids and death. Over the years, a new picture of the Vikings has slowly emerged. Archaeological discoveries have shown that the Vikings had a rich, vibrant culture that was in full flower by the time the first raids fell on the heads of the unsuspecting English monks. Far from being evil and barbaric, the Vikings were masters of technology, international trade, and law.

Worldwide Influence

Although the Vikings controlled many parts of Great Britain and Europe for only about three hundred years, they had a deep influence. They dominated many parts of Northern Europe for years. Viking settlers to Great Britain brought new ideas, such as the beginnings of the feudal system of government that became the norm long after the Vikings' influence faded. The Vikings created and founded market towns. They introduced new ideas about law and justice that became the foundation for many modern justice systems. They discovered vast new lands such as Greenland and Iceland with little more than their small, open boats and the spirit of adventure.

Another Viking contribution to the world was their vast experience in navigation and international trade. The Vikings traveled farther west than any known Europeans had ever done before, and they were the first to land in the New World—more than four hundred years before Christopher Columbus saw its shores. In the east, the Vikings influenced trade, creating international market towns where goods flowed throughout the world. The Vikings went wherever they wanted to go, whenever the wanted to, and for centuries no one could stop them.

A Vanishing Culture

Slowly, however, the Vikings seemed to disappear. Warfare, settlement, and the arrival of Christian beliefs in Viking lands all combined to halt Viking expansion. By 1100, all of the grand, frightening Viking raids had stopped. Vikings who had settled in England, Ireland, and France were old, and their children had adopted local languages, customs, and names.

But the world never forgot the Vikings. In the 1200s an Icelandic historian named Snorri Sturluson realized that the wonderful Viking stories and myths (called sagas) he had heard as a child were disappearing. He decided to write them down so they would be preserved forever. His work, called *Heimskringla*, became a literary masterpiece.

The sagas in Sturluson's book contain hundreds of details about ordinary Viking life, such as food, clothes, farming, and law, showing that the Vikings were much more than warriors. Sturluson's work, combined with recent discoveries in archaeology, have begun to reveal a Viking civilization that valued honor and truth, was filled with rich literature, and had the power—if only for a brief time—to rule the world.

CHAPTER ONE

BEFORE THE VIKING AGE

The year 789 was a time of unease and uncertainty in England. The years before had been marked by a succession of kings who fought to claim their own lands within the country. Battles scarred the region, and no one felt safe. The small farming communities that dotted the countryside were left unprotected, and even the few large villages, such as London, felt the bite of political unrest.

One day, word came that a group of ships had been spotted off the coast of Portland, an area in southern England. The ships were thought to be traders carrying such things as glass beads, silks, wines, and other goods from faraway places. The news of the arriving traders must have come as a pleasant surprise to people weary of constant political unrest. Trading for a few days might be just the thing to take their minds off their troubles for a time.

When news of the ships got to the king of Wessex, he sent a representative named Beaduheard to meet them. Beaduheard gathered a small band of men and hurried to Portland. No one knows how many ships or men greeted the small group of English that day. Researchers do know, however, that these strangers were not traders, and they cut down Beaduheard and his men with one stroke. These were Vikings, and this attack ushered in the Viking Age.

Such attacks took the people of England and Ireland completely by surprise. Few had ever heard of these wild, savage warriors who seemed to appear out of nowhere, slicing silently through the ocean on sleek boats. The Vikings landed on coastlines throughout Great Britain with no warning. They attacked undefended monasteries, looting treasures and killing inhabitants.

Who Were the Vikings?

The unexpectedness and swiftness of these attacks gave the Vikings an air of supernatural mystery. No one seemed to know who they were or where they came from. They appeared and disappeared as if by magic. No one knew when or where they would attack again. To the English, the Vikings were a terrible, bloodthirsty race of heathens sent by the devil to destroy God's work on earth.

The Vikings, however, were not supernatural beings created by the wrath of God. They came from an area far to the north of Europe, and were part of a civilization that had existed there for thousands of years. The Vikings' Scandinavian homeland consisted of three major areas that stretched for more than a thousand miles, areas we now call Denmark, Sweden, and Norway. It was in these cold lands that the Viking civilization rose, far from the knowledge of other European cultures.

Early Viking Culture

Although most Europeans did not know that the Viking civilization existed before the first Viking raid in England, scholars are certain that a rich and successful Viking civilization was thriving in Scandinavia long before the raids were recorded by terrified monks in the late eighth century. However, historians are unclear about how the earliest developments of the Viking culture really began. Very little information about this time in the Vikings' history has survived, primarily because the Vikings did not record their own history. As a result, most of the

Viking raiders landed on coastlines throughout Great Britain and with no warning, attacked undefended monasteries.

written records of the Vikings are from the people they attacked, which gives scholars a very biased view of the Vikings.

Thus, historians must piece together bits of information from a variety of sources to construct a picture of early Viking life. They look at such things as written evidence from outside cultures; Viking poetry and myths recorded centuries after the end of the Viking Age; Viking-era place-names in countries such as England and Ireland; and archaeo-logical finds in areas where the Vikings are known to have lived, such as Scandinavia, England, Ireland, Greenland, and Iceland, a large island northwest of Britain. Even with all of these sources, concrete information about the Vikings and the groups from which they developed is sadly lacking.

Scholars also look to the geography of Scandinavia itself for clues to the rise of the Viking civilization in the centuries before the Viking Age. The Vikings who made their

EARLY DESCRIPTIONS OF THE VIKINGS

Few Europeans recorded their earliest contacts with Vikings, so there is little information about the Vikings prior to the eighth century. However, a few ancient writings have survived. One of the oldest accounts comes from a Greek writer named Pytheas. Author P. H. Sawyer, in his book *Kings and Vikings: Scandinavia and Europe* A.D. *700–1100*, describes that in about 300 B.C. Pytheas wrote of a land he called Thule, where, "for lack of the crops and cattle of more genial lands, its inhabitants subsist on wild berries and 'millet' which they thresh in covered barns because of the continual rains. From the plentiful honey of their bees they prepare mead as a drink."

Three classical writers, including Pliny the Elder, Tacitus, and Ptolemy, also mentioned several early Viking tribes. They included, as historian David M. Wilson describes in his book, *The Vikings and Their Origins*, "the Suiones, who must almost certainly be the Swedes (Sviar) of Uppland who were to become the richest tribe in Scandinavia and whose territory was to be the kernel of the modern Swedish kingdom."

Tacitus also described the early people and culture of these northern lands. P. H. Sawyer says that Tacitus wrote, "The shape of their ships differs from the normal in having a prow at both ends, they do not rig sails or fasten their oars in banks at the side. . . .Wealth, too, is held in high honor. . . . Arms [weapons] are not, as in the rest of Germany, allowed to all and sundry, but kept under guard, and the guard is a slave."

homes in the cold countries to the north of Europe developed a way of life that was suited to the unique geography and climate of the Scandinavian countries. Historians believe that this climate and geography played a vital role in the rise of their civilization.

Geography and Its Effect on Early Viking Culture

The Vikings who lived in Scandinavia faced a number of imposing geographical features that affected their way of life. For example, water dominates many parts of Scandinavia, and the area is a peninsula filled with rivers, lakes, streams, bogs, and *fjords*—narrow inlets of the sea surrounded by steep cliffs. Other imposing geographical features include deep forests and impassable mountains. These features created barriers between the various groups of Vikings living throughout Scandinavia. As historians James Graham-Campbell and Dafydd Kidd suggest,

> Scandinavian geography is dominated by the sea and inland waterways and the possibilities they offer for communication. Because of the contrast between rich and poor agricultural land . . . [t]here are formed natural [logical] areas for settlement. Barriers to communication—forests, bogs, and mountains—dictate the relationship between those communities.[1]

Historians believe that the Vikings developed many aspects of their culture as a way to overcome the problems that the geography of the land presented. One of the hallmarks of the Viking civilization, for example, is their skill at navigation and shipbuilding. During

Because they needed to overcome various geographic barriers, the Vikings developed the most technologically advanced ships seen in Europe at the time.

the Viking Age, the Vikings had the most technologically advanced ships ever seen in Europe. Because of this fact, historians agree that they had developed their knowledge hundreds of years before they began raiding Europe. Further, scholars contend, the Vikings developed their skills at navigation and shipbuilding in Scandinavia because land travel would have been almost impossible in many areas of their homelands. The Vikings were forced to rely on water travel as their main means of communication and transportation. This enabled them to become skillful seamen and navigators—traits that would one day allow them to explore the world.

Although water dominated many areas of Scandinavia, other geographical features had a lasting effect on the Viking culture. Individual tribes lived in separate areas, and the lives of each tribe were influenced in a variety of ways by the local land, climate, and geography. Historian F. Donald Logan distinguishes the

For the Vikings of Norway, the many fjords in the region dictated their way of life.

three countries of Scandinavia and their geographical features, "If we are to look for a key to the geography of these places, it is in the mountains and fjords of Norway, the dense forestlands of Sweden, and the size of Denmark."[2]

Norway

The coastline of Norway extends more than sixteen hundred miles, making it one of the longest stretches of coast in Europe. The land is extreme, with hundreds of deep fjords and rocky mountains that are permanently covered with ice and snow. Fertile lands are squeezed between the mountains and the sea and along deep, shadowy valleys. The early Vikings settled in these narrow strips of farmable land near the fjords to make their living.

Although the area lies far to the north, the warm Gulf Stream ocean currents that originate in the Gulf of Mexico, move north in the Atlantic, and flow past Norway, give the land cool summers and mild winters. This made the area rich with wildlife such as reindeer, elk, wolf, bear, wolverine, and fox, which the Vikings hunted for meat and fur. The seas teemed with fish, whales, seals, and walrus. The Vikings who lived in this area were skilled hunters and trappers, and it is from Norway that much of the fur trade to Europe was established.

But it was the fjords that dictated life for the Vikings of Norway. Their settlements hugged the edges of fjords, some of which extended over a hundred miles into the interior of the land, and the people used them for transportation and communication. As Logan describes, "From fjord settlement to fjord settlement it was the highway of the sea that joined people together."[3]

Historians believe that the Vikings of Norway led the culture in developing navigational skills. Because they had to rely so heavily on water travel, it was vital that the people understand how to traverse large bodies of water safely.

Sweden

Deep, dense forests and waterways cover this area of Viking civilization. In the north, a mountainous area separates Sweden from Norway, making communication difficult between the groups of each area. The area has very cold winters with a great deal of ice and snow. In the south, the bogs and enormous woodlands make the area virtually impassable. Between these forests and waterways are small agricultural areas that are good for farming, and this is where many Vikings eventually settled.

Many of these settlements were separated by forests and water. People sought ways to communicate, trade, and interact with one another. They also sought out areas where communication was less difficult, areas that also saw a rise in trade settlements. One particular area of Sweden, called Uppland, was in a perfect place for settlement and trade. As Graham-Campbell and Kidd explain,

> Inland waters and ridges providing land routes made Uppland in east-central

Viking settlements in Sweden were separated by dense forests and water.

15

Sweden a natural center for early settlement. Its deep and protected inland waterway system gave Uppland access to the extensive Swedish coast and the rich Baltic islands of Oland and Gotland [other Viking areas] and accounts for the importance of the [large Viking settlement] sites Helgo, Birka and Sigtuna.[4]

Denmark

Compared with Sweden and Norway, Denmark is relatively small and very flat. The mainland of Denmark, called Jutland, does have many fjords along its eastern coastline. The flatness of the land and the lack of extreme geographical features such as mountains and vast waterways made Denmark good for agricultural development, with a climate of mild winters and warm summers. As a result, the Vikings who settled in Denmark were primarily a farming people. Although all the Vikings in Scandinavia farmed or herded animals, those in Denmark could take advantage of the fertile, flat land and the prime growing conditions of the climate.

The Danish Vikings were also in the best spot for trade and contact with the outside world. Jutland borders Germany, and this gateway enabled the Danish Vikings to interact with European cultures. As a result, some of Denmark's settlements, such as the town of Hedeby, became important trading centers later in the Viking Age. Through these, the Vikings of Denmark made contact with other cultures and became rich and powerful through trade. As author Else Roesdahl says,

As Scandinavia's southern gateway, Denmark had far more political and cultural contacts with its southern neighbors—Saxons, Frisians [a European culture] and Slavs—than Norway and Sweden, and many European influences reached it first. For sea-going traffic, Denmark was the gateway between the Baltic [Sea] on one side and the North Sea on the other.[5]

Early Viking Settlements and Society

All of these factors influenced the Vikings who dominated Europe during their golden age, but many people wonder about the cultures that came before the Vikings. Although historians know very little about them, scholars have established some basic facts about early Viking civilization.

Based on archaeological finds, scientists believe that some kind of culture was thriving in Scandinavia during the Bronze Age. The Bronze Age, the stage of prehistoric cultural development when bronze was first used to create tools, weapons, and other objects, began at different times in different areas of the world; it came to Denmark around 1800 B.C. and lasted for about one thousand years.

Most of the information that exists about early Bronze Age cultures in Scandinavia is based on burial finds or in what scientists refer to as hoards. *Hoards* are piles of objects made of bronze and other precious metals that have been found either buried or deposited in watery areas such as bogs and swamps. Because similar objects have been found throughout Scandinavia, historians believe that the early cultures probably had contact with each other and with other cultures. Historians Colleen Batey, Helen Clarke, R. I. Page, and Neil S. Price comment,

VIKING LANDS DURING THE VIKING AGE

At the end of the Viking Age, in about 1075, a cleric, a type of monk, named Adam of Bremen set out to record the culture of the Vikings as part of a history for the archbishops of Hamburg. Adam described many aspects of Viking culture and the areas in which the Vikings lived. Although he does seem to exaggerate at times, historians consider this document to be fairly accurate. Historian Else Roesdahl, in her book *The Vikings*, quotes part of Adam's description of the lands,

"[Sweden is] shut in by exceedingly high mountains. . . . The Swedish country is extremely fertile; the land is rich in fruits and honey besides excelling all others in cattle raising, exceedingly happy in streams and woods, the whole region full of merchandise from foreign parts. . . . [Norway] is the farthest country of the world. . . . On account of the roughness of its mountains and the immoderate cold, Norway is the most unproductive of all the countries, suited only for herds. . . . The people make a living from their livestock by using the milk of the flocks or herds for food and the wool for clothing. . . . The Danes . . . are just as poor. . . . Poverty has forced them thus to go all over the world and from piratical raids they bring home in great abundance the riches of the lands."

Discoveries of bronze objects of a uniform type throughout Scandinavia show that there were contacts between north and south. . . . In the Bronze Age these contacts were apparently fostered by trade: raw materials, perhaps mainly hides and furs, were exchanged for copper and tin to make bronze locally, or for manufactured bronze weapons such as swords and axes which were imported from central Europe and the British Isles.[6]

In addition to these hoards, scientists have discovered a number of graves in Scandinavia that date to the Bronze Age. In some graves, hollowed-out oak tree trunks serve as coffins, and the body was usually buried with a number of personal objects such as razors and tweezers. In some cases, clothing has been preserved, hinting at what ancient Vikings might have worn long ago. A few graves also included grave goods, beautiful metal artifacts, such as bronze helmets, shields, and objects made of gold. These grave goods suggest that

During the later phases of Viking culture, weapons such as this highly decorated axe blade were made of iron.

ologists divide this period in Scandinavia into phases based on the material finds that they have discovered: the Early Iron Age, the Roman Iron Age, and the Migration Period.

The Early Iron Age

Scientists know almost nothing about the Vikings who lived during the Early Iron Age, which lasted from about 500 to 100 B.C., because few objects from this period have been found. However, evidence from ancient settlements in Denmark suggest that the population was increasing during this time. The Danish settlements have characteristics similar to those of Viking Age settlements, such as houses grouped around a central village square, which suggest that this ancient culture was one predecessor of the Vikings.

Archaeologists have also found objects used as votive, or religious, offerings to gods and goddesses, many of which were thrown into bogs and lakes. The *Cultural Atlas of the Viking World* declared, "The practice of making votive offerings and sacrifices in bogs and lakes continued throughout the Iron Age. By far the greater number of the recovered offerings are of weapons, pottery, or metal vessels containing food, and animals."[7] This practice also was common during the Viking Age, suggesting that the cultures shared a common belief system. Other than these few clues, though, little else is known.

The Roman Iron Age

The next phase of Viking culture, the Roman Iron Age, lasted from about the first through the fourth centuries A.D. During this time, Europe and Great Britain had been torn apart by centuries of migration and warfare, but the Vikings in Scandinavia had been spared invasion and conquest by

early Viking society included some kind of ruling class rich enough to afford such objects.

A few settlement sites have been discovered from this period as well. They indicate that Scandinavia before the Viking Age was filled with small farms and individual settlements. A typical early Viking farm usually consisted of a long, stone building that housed both people and cattle, and a number of smaller outbuildings surrounded by stone walls. Other than these scattered finds, little is left from the Vikings who lived during this period.

Thus, scholars look to the next stage of development, the Iron Age, when iron replaced bronze as the basic material for making weapons and other objects, for information about the cultures that came immediately before the Viking Age. The Iron Age in Scandinavia lasted for about fifteen hundred years. Archae-

foreign, mainly Roman, armies. Historians Graham-Campbell and Kidd explain, "Scandinavia never became part of the [Roman] Empire. In consequence, it never had imposed on it the towns, bureaucracy and latterly Christianity, which were features common to all the Roman provinces and which strongly influenced their later development."[8] Because of the remoteness of their lands, the Vikings had little contact with the rest of the classical world (ancient Greece and Rome). As a result, a unique culture and belief system evolved separate from the conquering Romans, who had the most influence on the world at the time.

Historians are not completely sure why the Romans did not invade Scandinavia. Some speculate that the long distances to Viking lands were too daunting for Roman armies. Others suggest that the climate and geography of Scandinavia, with its vast waterways, bogs, and rocky mountains, dissuaded many

THE ORB OF THE WORLD

In the thirteenth century, an Icelandic scholar named Snorri Sturluson wrote down many of the Viking myths and stories for the first time. One of them, called the *History of the Kings of Norway*, includes a poetic and majestic description of the world according to the Vikings. Snorri wove stories about mythology in with the actual history of the Vikings, creating a document that was part fiction, part historical fact. For example, he lists the various kings of Norway but begins by saying that they were all descended from the Viking god Odin. Historian Magnus Magnusson writes in his book *Vikings!* that the work is also known as *Heimskringla* (or Orb of the World) from its first line:

"The orb of the world, which mankind inhabits, is riven [overrun] by many fjords, so the great seas run into the land from the Outer Ocean. Thus, it is known that a great sea goes through Norvadund [Straits of Gibraltar] all the way to the land of Jerusalem. . . . Through Greater Sweden [Russia], from the range of mountains that lie to the north beyond the edge of human habitation, there runs a river properly called the Tanais [Don], which flows into the Black Sea. In Asia to the east of the Tanais there was a land called Asaland or Asaheim [Land of the Aesir, the Viking gods], its chief city was called Asgard [Home of the Aesir]. That city was ruled by a chieftain called Odin."

would-be invaders from attempting conquest. Regardless of the reason, the Romans did not attack but instead, began trading with the Scandinavians.

This trade relationship deeply affected the early Viking civilization. The people began to realize the potential for wealth and power through trade with Rome, and it wasn't long before their culture thrived on the wealth and prestige of Roman goods. According to historian P. H. Sawyer,

> The artifacts that reached Scandinavia [during the Roman Iron Age] were generally luxury goods, made by craftsmen rather than mass produced. There are many glass bowls and beakers, cauldrons and other large bronze vessels, jugs, bowls, ladles of silver or bronze, jewelry, fine pottery

and weapons. . . . [S]ome reached Scandinavia by way of trade, in exchange for northern goods such as amber [a precious stone created from fossilized tree sap] and furs that were in demand in the Roman Empire.[9]

According to historians, the Viking economy began to rely more and more on the wealth that trading offered. During this period, settlements and farms grew, new land was settled, and some Viking settlements even became trading centers where goods from around the world could be found. This influx of wealth, scholars believe, must have created a need for some kind of political or social structure, which in turn would have stirred the beginnings of social and political organization that would eventually become Viking law and government.

Pictured are Roman glass bowls, beakers, and bronze vessels. Soon after their first contact with the Romans, the Vikings began to see the potential for wealth and power through trade with Rome.

Although the Romans ruled the world for centuries, however, their power was not to last. With their demise came the disappearance of the Vikings from the consciousness of most of Europe during the next significant phase of early Viking civilization.

The Migration Period

The Migration Period lasted from about the fifth to the sixth centuries A.D. and was a time of decline and turmoil. By the end of the fourth century A.D., Germanic tribes swept through Europe, defeating Roman armies and causing the collapse of the once-great Roman Empire. Local governments crumbled, trade halted, and communities were left undefended and vulnerable to attack. The Germanic invaders carved up Europe, eventually creating hundreds of small kingdoms ruled by individual kings and chieftains who were constantly at war with one another. In other places, settlements were abandoned, creating large tracts of uninhabited areas and the mass movement of thousands of people in Europe.

Although historians believe that the Vikings did not migrate during this time, the defeat of the Roman Empire still had a devastating effect on them because their economy had relied on the exchange of goods with Rome. When the Germanic tribes overwhelmed Europe, the once-rich trade relationship between the Vikings and the Romans vanished, and the demand for their goods in Europe declined dramatically.

Although historians suspect that the early Germanic tribes continued to trade with the Vikings, the quantities were much smaller than before the Roman collapse. Most historians think that this caused an economic collapse in the Viking culture. Many Scandinavian settlements were abandoned, and the poor condition of Viking graves from this time suggests that the culture was in decline.

Evidence also suggests that the Vikings experienced warfare and political unrest in their homelands. Many archaeological finds from the era include buried treasures of precious objects, which historians believe were personal fortunes that people hid from danger. Historian Edvard Henriksen describes this, saying, "About A.D. 500 the . . . farms were deserted, many of them burnt down, and at the same time huge treasures of jewelry and gold coins were dug into the ground, sure sign of war. From the same period are also a number of fortified encampments on Öland [an area of Scandinavia]."[10]

From the sixth through the eighth centuries, the Vikings virtually disappeared from European recorded history. Later, though, in the last decades before the beginning of the Viking Age, rich grave finds and archaeological digs in Scandinavia show that the Viking culture had once again risen to prominence. Scholars believe that, in the two hundred years before the Viking Age, the Viking civilization was experiencing movement and change. Trade communities grew, and powerful families vied for power and the precious land that came with it. The land prospered; agriculture became more productive; and trade expanded. All of these factors combined to create an atmosphere of security and self-confidence that pervaded Viking society at the beginning of the Viking Age.

However, there is no information to tell historians how the Vikings recovered from the years of hardship or when their society began to become stronger. They were still, for the most part, anonymous to the rest of Europe.

CHAPTER TWO

RAIDS AND WARFARE

The Vikings burst into European consciousness abruptly in 789 and took everyone by surprise. Because the attacks seemed so random, the mere threat of one kept people fearful and on edge.

At the time, no one knew why the warriors began attacking, but modern scholars believe that the Vikings had specific reasons. The last years before the beginning of the Viking Age were a volatile time in Viking history, and historians speculate that three factors led the Vikings to begin raiding: overpopulation of Viking lands, political turmoil, and the overriding desire for honor and wealth that pervaded Viking culture.

Overpopulation

Many historians suspect that an explosion in the Viking population was one reason that the Vikings set out to find new lands. Historians are unclear as to when, why, or how the problem of overpopulation began, but archaeological remains of Viking towns suggest that the population was growing in the decades before the Viking Age.

This was a particular problem for the Vikings, who based their system of honor and power on land ownership. The people who controlled the arable land had a great deal of power and prestige in society. As the popula-

tion grew, the amount of available land to control was divided into smaller and smaller parcels. Thus, young men who needed land and wealth to achieve power had to seek it beyond the borders of their Scandinavian homelands. According to seventeenth-century writer Sir William Temple, "Each of these countries [Denmark, Sweden, and Norway] was like a mighty [bee] hive, which, by the vigor of propagation and health of the climate, growing too full of people, threw out some new swarm at certain periods of time, that took wing, and sought out some new abode."[11]

This surge in population was due, some scholars believe, to the practice of polygamy—having more than one mate—that some suspected was a part of Viking society during the years just prior to the beginning of the Viking Age. This theory, put forth by an eleventh-century Norman cleric named Dudo, contends that

> These people who insolently abandon themselves to excessive indulgence, live in outrageous union with many women and there in shameless and unlawful intercourse breed innumerable progeny [offspring]. Once they have grown up, the young quarrel violently

with their fathers and grandfathers, or with each other, about property, and if they increase too greatly in number, and cannot acquire sufficient arable land to live on, a large group is selected by the drawing of lots according to ancient custom. . . . [The losers] are driven away to foreign peoples and realms, so that they by fighting can gain themselves countries where they can live in continual peace.[12]

Although modern historians disagree about whether the Vikings actually practiced polygamy, it is clear that something initiated a rise in the Viking population. This, in turn, compelled many to set out for new lands.

Political Turmoil

Another reason some Vikings left their homeland had to do with internal warfare and political strife. Although little information exists detailing the conflicts within Viking society in the years prior to the Viking Age, historians believe that the Viking culture was constantly shifting as chieftains and local kings fought one another for land and power.

Historians point to one specific political event, the rise of Harald Fairhair in Norway, that may have caused such political upheaval. In the late 800s, Harald attempted to unify the land and set himself up as ruler of Norway. According to Viking stories called sagas, many Norwegian chieftains who did not want to be subjected to Harald's rule left to settle new lands elsewhere.

Furthermore, many historians maintain that the Viking spirit also led to people leaving. Known for independence and individuality, the Viking people constantly quarreled among themselves, fought one another for land, and vied for positions

Because Viking attacks appeared to be random, the mere threat of one kept people fearful and on edge.

DESCRIPTION OF A VIKING FLEET

The mere sight of a Viking ship on the horizon could strike fear in anyone who saw it coming, and it became the terrifying image of Viking attack for many Europeans during the early part of the Viking Age. But the beauty and splendor of these ships also awed those who saw them. Jacqueline Simpson, in her book *Everyday Life in the Viking Age*, relates one eyewitness description of a Viking fleet:

"So great also was the ornamentation of the ships that the eyes of the beholders were dazzled, and to those looking from afar they seemed to be of flame rather than of wood. . . . Gold shone on the prows, silver also flashed on the variously shaped ships. So great, in fact, was the magnificence of the fleet, that if its lord had desired to conquer any peoples, the ships alone would have terrified the enemy, before the warriors whom they carried joined battle at all."

in the local governments. Many who lost these internal battles found themselves either banished or stripped of their lands and wealth. These men then decided to leave Scandinavia to find their own way in the outside world. Early medieval historians who recorded events of the time said, "Chieftains, sons of kings, or pretenders to the throne left their homelands because the opportunities were better abroad or they were exiled."[13]

Honor and Wealth

Regardless, the most compelling reason that many Vikings struck out from their homes, suggest historians, was a simple desire for power, honor, and wealth. Many early European sources indicate that the Vikings first sought easy money, pillaging the wealthy Christian monasteries and taking the riches

back to Scandinavia. They then used this new wealth to build power and status in their own country. Eventually, some Vikings established permanent bases in England and Ireland, slowly moving to the new lands permanently, to trade and farm.

Vikings had a long trading history, first with Rome and then with Europe's Germanic tribes, and this gave them a taste of the life that wealth and commerce could bring. Many trading centers had been established in the coastal areas of Western Europe, England, the Baltic regions, and Russia. Far more goods were being traded, which meant much more plunder for the Vikings to trade—or to steal.

All of these factors contributed to the fact that, by the end of the 700s, the Vikings were ready to explore the world and take advantage of the riches that could be found there. They would do it, at first, by attacking and raiding the nearby areas of England and Ireland.

First Viking Raids

Most historians believe that the first raids on England and Ireland came from Vikings in Norway, to be followed in later years by Vikings from Sweden and Denmark. And in many cases, groups of Vikings from several different areas of Scandinavia eventually joined forces and attacked the English coastlines.

Little is known of the Vikings who first plundered England, because they left no written records of their exploits. No records explain why the Vikings chose England and Ireland as their targets, although historians speculate it was because those areas are rela-

tively close to the Norwegian coast, with easy access by sea.

Regardless of their reasons, the Vikings saw these raids as an opportunity for adventure, to see new lands and battle enemies. For the most part, the Viking civilization was not an overly violent culture. But the people believed in personal strength, glory, and warfare. As a result, they used battle to attain wealth, political power, and fame.

Lindisfarne

Although the first record of a Viking attack came in 789, it was another Viking raid four years later that shook England—and eventually, the rest of the world—to its intellectual and spiritual core.

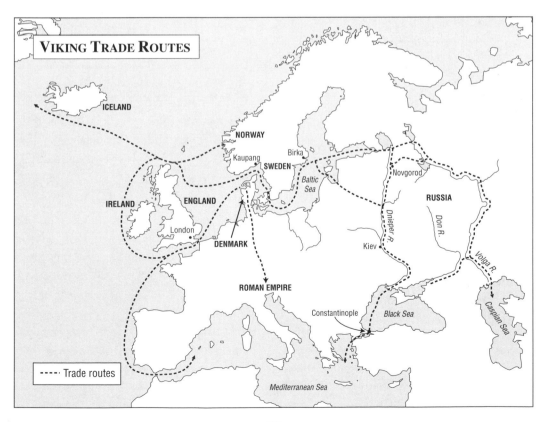

VIKING TRADE ROUTES

---- Trade routes

In the year 793, England was a green and peaceful land. Small settlements dotted the coastlines, and learning and literature flourished in the Christian monasteries. The monasteries were the houses of god, but they also housed libraries containing huge, hand-lettered books decorated with gold and precious jewels, golden cups and chalices, silver plates, carved ivory objects, decorated weapons, beautiful metalwork, delicate embroideries, and rich fabrics. All of these objects were used in the worship of the Christian god, and people throughout the land considered them to be sacred. They were safe from attack, the people believed, for they were protected by god himself.

As it turned out, these monasteries were not immune to attack after all. On June 8, 793, the people realized this when the Vikings attacked the monastery at Lindisfarne. The *Anglo-Saxon Chronicle*, a historical text that documents events during the Viking Age, describes the events of that year in a mythical way, saying,

> In this year terrible portents [signs] appeared over Northumbria which sorely affrighted the inhabitants: there were exceptional flashes of lightning, and fiery dragons were seen flying through the air. A great famine followed hard upon these signs; and a little later in that same year, on the 8th of June, the harrying [harassing] of the heathen miserably destroyed God's Church on Lindisfarne by rapine [plunder] and slaughter.[14]

The attack on Lindisfarne was a special horror to Christians. An early church had been founded there more than two hundred years before, and in 687 a famous Christian

saint, St. Cuthbert, had been buried there. For two centuries, Christians considered Lindisfarne an especially holy and respected place. So the Viking attack there felt, to the Christians, like an attack on god himself.

The raid on Lindisfarne also had an enormous impact on England and the world, which is why historians consider it to be the official beginning of the Viking Age. Because Lindisfarne was a major center of Christian learning, the Viking attack was devastating news. One contemporary account describes the devastation that the Vikings wrought:

> And they [the Vikings] came to the church of Lindisfarne, laid everything waste with grievous plundering, trampled the holy places with polluted feet, dug up the altars and seized all the treasures of the holy church. They killed some of the brothers [monks]; some they took away with them in fetters; many they drove out, naked and loaded with insults; and some they drowned in the sea.[15]

Most of the information about the Viking raid on Lindisfarne comes from English written sources, and one of the most fascinating is a series of letters written by a scholar named Alcuin from the English kingdom of Northumbria. He was so upset at the attack that he wrote many letters describing the raid. One of them said,

> Never before has such terror appeared in Britain as we have now suffered from a pagan [non-Christian] race; nor was it thought that such an

ANGLO-SAXON CHRONICLE

The *Anglo-Saxon Chronicle* is considered to be one of the most important historical writings in Europe. The *Chronicle* is really a collection of several texts that record the history of England from the first through about the middle of the twelfth centuries, added to by monks and other Christians for hundreds of years. It is the earliest known history of a European group written in the people's own language.

However, the people who laboriously recorded the battles, raids, and other events of their time were not historians. Their purpose was only to set down facts and dates so that others could follow the passage of time by marking what happened in each year. As a result, there is no commentary or explanation of the events recorded in the *Chronicle*, but only dates and brief mentions of the most newsworthy happenings in any given year.

Many of these events were Viking raids and attacks, and some sections of the *Chronicle* focus almost exclusively on the conflict between the English and the Vikings. The sheer number of mentions of Viking raids in the *Chronicle* suggests to scholars that these raids were extremely significant.

The entries in the *Chronicle* are an invaluable record to historians and scholars who study Viking history. There is one terse entry from A.D. 837:

"This year Alderman Wulfherd fought at Hamton with thirty-three pirates [Vikings], and after great slaughter obtained the victory, but he died the same year. Alderman Ethelhelm also, with the men of Dorsetshire, fought with the Danish army in Portland-isle, and for a good while put them to flight; but in the end the Danes became masters of the field, and slew the alderman."

inroad from the sea could be made. Behold, the church of St. Cuthbert spattered with the blood of the priests of god, despoiled of all its ornaments, a place more venerable than all in Britain is given as prey to pagan peoples.[16]

Raids on Ireland

By 795, the first wave of Viking raids in England ceased. For about the next thirty years, until the 830s, the Vikings raided Ireland instead. Ireland, a country divided into many small independent kingdoms, could not organize any kind of group resistance to the Viking

Pictured are the ruins of the monastery at Lindisfarne, which was attacked by Vikings on June 8, 793.

onslaught. Also, Ireland was a Christian country with many monasteries that contained the same kinds of wealth and treasure that the Vikings had found in England.

Although little specific information exists about the early Viking raids, one Irish document called the *Annals of Ulster* recorded the Viking attacks by listing what areas were plundered. According to the *Annals*, in 794 Vikings attacked an area of Ireland called the Hebrides and also perhaps south of that. The *Annals* specifically point to Viking raids in 795 on the islands of Skye and Iona off the western coast of Scotland, the island of Lambay north of Dublin, and two islands called Inishmurray and Inishbofin off the Irish coast.

Three years later, Vikings attacked and plundered the Irish island of Inispatrick. For the next few years, the Viking attacks continued: Iona again in 802 and in 806, when sixty-eight people were killed by the Northmen. In 812, areas known as the Owles of Mayo and Connemara were attacked, and the Owles were attacked again the next year. The large, wealthy monastery in the area of Armaugh was plundered three times in one month in the year 832.

Why They Attacked Churches

In each instance the Vikings pillaged churches, stole valuables, and captured people to sell into slavery. The Irish were appalled that the Vikings raided their sacred churches, denouncing the Northmen as demon heathens. The monks and other Christians believed the Vikings had set out to destroy the Christian faith by sacking its monasteries and churches.

But the Vikings did not concentrate on the monasteries because they wanted to wipe out Christianity. Most historians suggest that the Vikings did not think of religion at all as they plundered the rich Christian buildings in England, Ireland, and elsewhere. They concentrated on these places because the best loot could be found in the monasteries. The areas around some monasteries were also attractive to Vikings looking for quick riches because, as historian Roesdahl notes, "Several monasteries were . . . important economic and political centers, sometimes with many inhabitants, where much wealth might be accumulated or stored. They were so well organized that they could survive attacks [and recover] and could thus be plundered again and again."[17]

For more than thirty years, the Vikings continued to attack Ireland. They took not only religious objects, but also any small objects that caught their eye. Many of these found their way back to Scandinavia, where they were found by archaeologists centuries later. As Roesdahl says, "A great quantity of such items, torn from reliquaries [containers that held religious artifacts], sacred books and other church objects in Ireland . . . ended up in graves in Norway. Some were no doubt taken home as souvenirs and given to wives and girlfriends and some were refashioned as jewelry."[18]

Fleets of ships like the one shown here in a museum enabled the Vikings to plunder the coasts of Europe with little opposition.

Little could be done to stop the Vikings, although occasionally an Irish army managed to put up a small fight. The Vikings were virtually undefeatable because they had a secret weapon that no one in Europe had ever seen: Fast, sleek ships. It was these ships that enabled the Vikings to carry out years of plundering with little opposition.

Viking Ships

The grand Viking ships, with their carvings of ferocious dragons at the prow, have become a symbol of the Viking Age. It was the ships that enabled the Vikings to strike without warning from places that no one had ever dreamed an attack could come. According to

In Norway, a fierce dragon's head tops the prow of a modern-day reproduction of a Viking ship.

historian Johannes Brondsted, "The ships of the Vikings were the supreme achievement of their technical skill, the pinnacle of their material culture; they were the foundation of their power, their delight, and their most treasured possessions."[19]

Centuries of life in the water-filled world of Scandinavia helped the Vikings develop sophisticated methods of water transportation. The technology of their ships evolved over many years and was the high point in their achievement. Those ships gave the Vikings the ability to attack with lightning-fast speed.

The hallmark of the Viking ship was that it could sail in shallow water, whereas all other ships of the day needed deep water. Viking ships were built long and shallow, not much of the boat dipped under water, and this design enabled the Vikings to sail right up on a beach or quietly up a shallow river. No other boats during this time could do this. Historians Graham-Campbell and Kidd explain,

> [The ships'] construction . . . allowed [the Vikings] to use any sloping beach as their harbor and to maneuver in waters unsuitable for most European vessels of that time. No wonder that surprise was felt, along with terror and rage, at such raids, for it was not just islands, like Lindisfarne, or coastal settlements that suffered at the hands of Vikings. They rowed their ships up rivers that led them to rich inland cities and monasteries . . . . That the Viking Age in western Europe began when it did must be attributed largely to the development of such ships in Scandinavia during the eighth century.[20]

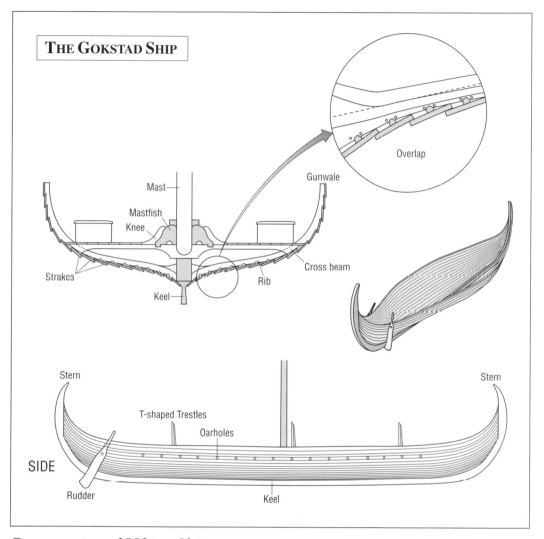

THE GOKSTAD SHIP

Overlap

Mast

Gunwale

Mastfish

Knee

Strakes

Cross beam

Keel

Rib

Stern

Stem

T-shaped Trestles

Oarholes

SIDE

Rudder

Keel

Construction of Viking Ships

Due to a variety of spectacular archaeological finds, researchers know a great deal about the construction of ships during the Viking Age. Some Vikings were buried within full-sized ships, and some of these burial mounds have been excavated, revealing a wealth of information.

One of the most famous Viking ships is the Gokstad, which was found and excavated in the late 1800s. Made entirely of strong oak, the ship is about seventy-six feet long, over seventeen feet wide, and more than six feet deep. The keel, a strip of wood stretching along the entire bottom of the boat, was shaped from a single piece of oak. Each end of the boat, the stem (front) and the stern (rear), rise in beautiful curves.

The hull, or bottom of the boat, is made of sixteen rows of planking called strakes. Most of the strakes are about one inch thick. These overlap each other and are attached to one another with iron rivets. They are also attached

31

to a set of wooden ribs that make up the internal structure of the boat. The strakes that would be below the water are tied to the ribs with spruce roots, another Viking trademark, instead of being nailed to the ribs. This makes the boat much more flexible in the water, an innovation that enabled Viking sailors to maneuver safely through rough waters with ease.

The ship's tall mast held a large, squarish sail. These sails were another important innovation of the Vikings. Sails had been used by previous cultures, and historians are uncertain exactly when the Vikings began using them. But when the Vikings added sails to their light, strong boats, they created a mighty combination of strength and speed that made Viking ships a marvel of the time. Historian Roesdahl says,

> Sails seem to have been introduced during the centuries preceding the Viking Age, although sailing ships had then been used in Western Europe for many hundreds of years. In Scandi-

navia sailing ships rapidly attained a level of sophistication that was outstanding for their time. Without sails, the far-flung exploits of the Vikings would have been impossible.[21]

Another new technique that Vikings used in their ships was a side rudder. In most ships, the rudder is a huge oarlike mechanism at the back of the boat that steers the ship. However, the Vikings put rudders along the right side of their ships. This helped stabilize the ships in the water, making them much more maneuverable and allowed the Vikings to sail into areas that other ships could not explore. The position of the rudder also created a common nautical word, starboard, (steer-board) which now refers to the right side of any ship.

When the winds were not favorable for sailing, Vikings rowed their boats with long oars that were fitted along the sides of the boat. This combination of sail and oar on one boat was yet another unique example of

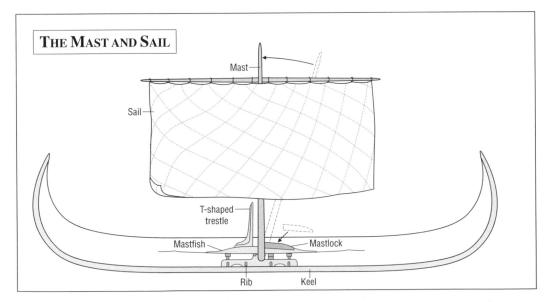

THE MAST AND SAIL

Mast

Sail

T-shaped trestle

Mastfish

Mastlock

Rib

Keel

Viking ingenuity. It gave the boats a great advantage because the Vikings could row up rivers and maneuver their vessels in difficult winds and currents.

Not only were Viking ships a technological wonder, but they were also decorated with magnificent objects, gold, and weapons. Many ships had elaborately carved prows of dragons and other fanciful beasts. Gold and silver ornaments decorated parts of a Viking ship, and much of the wood was carved into beautiful designs.

Everyone who saw a Viking ship slicing purposefully through the water toward them knew that an attack was imminent. Soon a mighty host of fierce Viking warriors, with their strong weapons and armor, would wreak havoc on the area.

Weaponry

Little information exists on how the Viking armies were amassed in Scandinavia during the Viking Age. Historians do know, however, that there was no such thing as a warrior caste, or group, in Viking society. Every Viking man was a warrior. Any farmer or craftsman could at any time join a roving band of raiders for a summer of plundering along the English coastline, or to fight a rival chieftain's followers in Scandinavia. Other groups of men gathered their weapons and went in search of new lands, which they would seize by warfare. Even in times of peace, feuds and infighting among members of Viking tribes kept most people well practiced in warfare.

Thus, a Viking's weapons were his most valuable possessions. He was usually buried with them, and most Vikings rarely went anywhere without being armed. One Viking poem illustrated this attitude with the words,

In the fields no man should stir one step
　From where his weapons are,
For it's hard to tell when he'll need a spear
　As he walks out on his way.[22]

Swords and Spears

A Viking's most important weapon was his sword. Thousands of Viking swords have been excavated by archaeologists, which suggests their importance to Viking society. Although the Vikings used many different kinds of swords, most were long, one-handed slashing swords. Some Viking blades were single edged, but most had sharp edges on both sides of the blade. The Vikings carried their swords in scabbards, or holders, made of wood and leather, usually lined with wool or other fabric. Many scabbards were highly decorated with carvings, metalwork, and gems.

Spears were also a popular Viking weapon. Most spears had blades about eighteen inches long, and some were decorated with precious metals like silver. Many Vikings used a combination of sword and spear during a fight. Later, they began to use axes instead of spears, and eventually axes became the typical weapon of the Vikings. By the end of the Viking Age, axes were often considered to be a cheaper alternative to the combination of the sword and spear, which was usually still the preference of the richer and powerful Viking warriors.

Armor

Historians are not sure exactly what kind of body armor a Viking warrior wore because they have found very few examples of armor in Viking burials. However, many Viking stories mention chain mail, a long shirt made of tiny interlocking rings. A few fragments of chain mail have survived, which suggest that some Vikings might have worn such shirts.

VIKING SWORDS

A Viking warrior's sword was his most prized possession. Grand swords were given as gifts, and some were even handed down from father to son. Swords were also celebrated in Viking poetry and stories and were called by many different names, as historians Peter G. Foote and David M. Wilson describe in their book, *The Viking Achievement*.

"A vast number of kennings [names] were invented for them [swords]— 'fire of battle,' 'lightning flash of blood,' 'snake of wounds,' 'icicle of the baldric.' Many were given names, often based on the quality of the swords themselves: *Brynjubitr* (Byrnie [a short coat of chain mail armor]-biter), *Fotbitr* (Leg-biter), *Gramr* (Fierce), *Gullinhjati* (Gold-hilt), *Hvati* (Keen or sharp), *Langhvass* (Long-and-sharp), or *Miofainn* (Ornamented-down-the-middle)."

Swords, such as these with their ornamented handles, were prized possessions of the Vikings.

However, most Vikings probably wore leather armor instead, mainly because it was cheaper than chain mail. Scholars suspect that other Vikings might have sewn bone plates inside their clothing for protection.

Historians are more certain that Vikings wore some type of helmet during battle. In fact, one of the most recognizable Viking symbols is the famous two-horned helmet, although historians suspect that these were used only in religious rituals. Scholars point to pictures and rock carvings that show Vikings wearing small round caps made of leather or metal, with a straight nosepiece down the front.

Most Vikings also carried round shields about three feet in diameter that were made to protect the body from the chin to the knee. They were usually made of brightly painted wood reinforced at the edges with more wood or metal. According to Roesdahl, "Yellow and black shields were found on the Gokstad ship, red shields are mentioned in contemporary literature, and *Ragnarsdrapa*—the earliest surviving scaldic [Viking style] poem—describes a shield painted with pictures from popular stories of gods and heroes."[23]

For more than forty years, the Vikings used their ships and their weapons against the undefended monasteries and settlements of England and Ireland. Their lightning raids on unsuspecting areas created a climate of fear. Their amazing ships enabled them to attack with deathly speed, landing without warning, yet the Vikings were not interested in creating fear. They did not really even want to control the people they attacked. Instead, the attacks were made simply to gain wealth and glory in their homelands.

Chapter Three

SETTLING DOWN

For decades, the Vikings attacked undefended monasteries in England and Ireland and plundered the riches they found there. Slowly, however, their purpose began to change. Instead of seeing England and Ireland as a source of wealth to take back to Scandinavia, the Vikings began settling in the new areas permanently.

The Last Raids

But the change from marauding armies to settlers and farmers came slowly. For about thirty years, from 793 to the 830s, the Vikings continued their raids, concentrating on Ireland and leaving England alone. By the 830s, however, the Vikings began attacking England once again. Scholars do not know why the Vikings turned their attention back to England, but historians Coleen Batey, Helen Clarke, R. I. Page, and Neil S. Price describe the new Viking attacks:

The 830s saw the Scandinavians take a renewed interest in England. . . . A large Danish force landed in 835 on the isle of Sheppy in the Thames [River] estuary from where they ravaged the surrounding area. From then on until about 850 the south coast [of England] was devastated by a series of attacks, including raids on London and Rochester, Kent. Pitched battles

were fought with the Vikings in Dorset and at Southampton and raids were also carried out on the east coast in the kingdom of Lindsey and farther north in Northumbria.[24]

Usually, the raiders attacked in the warm summer months, when travel to and from Scandinavia was easy. The English and Irish could breathe easier in the fall and winter, when they knew the Vikings would be far away in their own lands. Historians relate,

The raiding fleets had been a purely seasonal phenomenon plundering during the summer as the opportunity arose and then returning to Scandinavia for the winter; the raiders also remained highly mobile, their success stemming in part from . . . the capabilities of their longships, which enabled them to mount sudden attacks deep inland along the river systems then withdraw with the loot before an organized retaliation could be launched.[25]

This all changed in 850. That year, an army of Vikings camped on the island of Thanet at the mouth of the Thames River all winter. That winter represented a new phase in Viking culture. Raiding was no longer a strictly seasonal occupation; it was becoming a way of life.

First Settlements in England

The English were horrified that the once-sporadic Viking raids had become a permanent part of their lives. As historian Magnusson relates, "The character of the Viking incursions [invasions] had now changed drastically, and for the worse from the English point of view. The Danes had abandoned their ships as their major or sole means of transport and become a land force, well mounted [on horseback] and highly mobile."[26]

For the first few years, the Vikings lived in large military camps. They attacked nearby settlements, plundering their riches, before establishing new camps elsewhere. In 865, however, they hit upon a brand-new and much safer way to take wealth. They began to demand a sum of money, called danegeld, from the English. In return, the Vikings promised not to attack a particular settlement or area.

Many English settlements paid the money, hoping desperately that the Vikings would not attack them. But paying danegeld was no guarantee that the Vikings would not attack anyway. After the people of Kent paid a Viking army not to attack, for example, the

Viking raiding fleets usually attacked England and Ireland during the warm summer months when travel was easy.

Anglo-Saxon Chronicle relates, "under the cover of that peace and promise of money the [Viking] army stole away inland by night and ravaged all eastern Kent."[27]

The Coming of the Viking Armies

In 866, an enormous Viking army arrived in England. The *Anglo-Saxon Chronicle* described it as *micel here*, an unclear phrase that many historians translate as Great Army. This Viking army numbered somewhere between five hundred and two thousand, although historians dispute the exact numbers. The warriors had come to England for the express purpose of winning English lands to settle. For the next few years, the Great Army worked its way through England, conquering small areas, harassing local settlements, and eventually acquiring a great deal of land.

The Great Army was not the only one to begin an invasion for land and settlement. Other Viking armies had also begun to settle north, in Ireland. In 840, a fleet of Viking ships that had raided near the Irish area of Lough Neagh did not return home for the winter. A few Viking camps were established in Ireland in 841, and for the next few years, Viking armies used them as a base to attack the surrounding countryside. Eventually the Vikings in Ireland built more permanent settlements and also began demanding danegeld from their Irish victims. According to an Irish record called

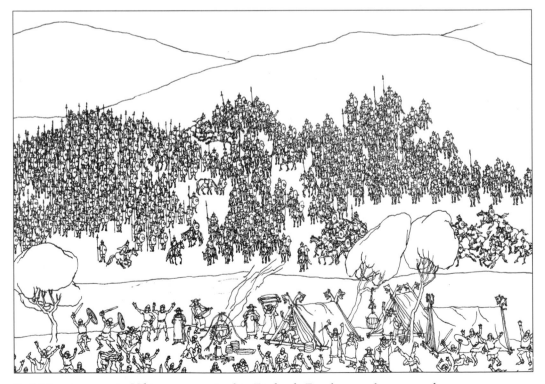

In 866, an enormous Viking army arrived in England. For the next few years, the army conquered small areas, set up camps, and harassed local settlements.

38

the *Annals of St. Bertin* in 847, "The Irish, who had been attacked by the Northmen for a number of years, were made into regular tribute-payers. The Northmen also got control of the islands all around Ireland, and stayed there without encountering any resistance from anyone."[28]

Moving Into France

It was much the same in France. During the years that the Viking raiders attacked areas of Ireland and England, some Viking ships also attacked places in what is now France. By the year 840, two Vikings were in military service to the French king Louis the Pious, and they and their families were given lands in France and lived there until about 885. During this time, a group of Vikings led by a leader named Hasting sailed up the Loire River into France. Members of this group took their wives and children and settled in an area called Angers. Throughout this time, other Viking groups continued to raid and attack French settlements in their quest for land to call their own.

Furthermore, the Great Army of Vikings that had first landed in England also moved south into France. They attacked many French settlements as they moved, prompting one fearful ancient historian to write,

> The northmen continue to kill and take Christian people captive; without ceasing they destroy churches and dwellings and burn towns. Along all the roads one sees bodies of the clergy and laity [nonclergy], of nobles and others, of women, children, and infants. There is no road on which the bodies of the slain Christians are not strewn. Sorrow and despair fill the hearts of all Christians who witness this.[29]

Modern scholars suspect that these and other accounts of the Vikings in Europe are highly exaggerated, but they capture some of the fear and uncertainty that the Viking raids and armies caused throughout the world as they searched for land on which to settle. Whether or not the accounts are accurate, it is clear that the Vikings did eventually make their homes in many areas of France. Eventually, these became known as the lands of the Northmen, or Normandy, a name still used today, a link to the area's Viking history.

Settling the Danelaw

Despite the fact that they settled in foreign lands, the Vikings did not want to conquer governments or become rulers of countries. They just wanted land, wealth, and prestige. In most cases, the Vikings met with little resistance from local lords or chieftains. They fought these minor leaders until they were able to secure enough land to establish farms and trade settlements.

Sometimes, however, the Vikings did fight large, difficult battles against mighty kings. One such king was Alfred the Great of England. Alfred had spent many years battling the Great Army when it landed in England and tried to settle in his kingdom of Wessex. The fighting was long and bitter, until finally Alfred agreed to a treaty with a Viking leader named Gunthrum. The treaty, called the Treaty of Wedmore, gave the Vikings the northern half of England if they promised to be loyal to Alfred as the king of England.

The Vikings agreed, and this area of England became known as the Danelaw, named for the Danes, or Vikings, who settled there.

Alfred the Great, the English king who helped establish the Danelaw.

The Vikings immediately introduced their laws, customs, and lifestyles to the Danelaw. And during the next few years, hundreds of Viking men, women, and children came from Scandinavia to make their homes there. Today, many modern towns and geographical areas in the Danelaw area of England still bear Scandinavian place-names, supporting the theory that large numbers of Vikings moved into the area. Historian F. Donald Logan explains, "The place-name . . . evidence as well as the linguistic [language] evidence suggest a very considerable Scandinavian colonization, and since the relatively small [original] armies cannot ex-

plain a settlement of such a great size, another immigration . . . must have occurred."[30]

Organizing Settlements

The Vikings who settled in the Danelaw and other parts of England had a very organized way of distributing and settling on their new lands, and this form of land distribution was completely new in England. First, Viking leaders gained control of huge tracts of land for settlement, dividing the English countryside into large rural estates. These estates could produce all the food and raw material that the new Viking inhabitants needed. Most of these estates included woodlands, pastures, fertile fields for crops, an abundance of water, and other resources.

The overlord who controlled the entire estate usually awarded small parts of the area to his loyal warriors and followers. The men who were given these smaller settlements did not own the land outright but were allowed to establish their own farms and to exploit whatever natural resources were available. In return, the overlord expected to receive a tribute, either in goods or services, from the warriors to whom he had given land. English citizens who still lived in the area were also expected to pay.

As a result of this method of land division, trading goods and services for land rights became common. Thus, the area saw a growth of trade and markets to which people from the surrounding areas traveled to buy goods. Some of the largest and most prosperous were in the

Danelaw, including the Viking town of Jorvik, which is now known as York.

York

Long before the Vikings began raiding and settling in England, York was a peaceful, settled community. When the Great Army of the Vikings moved through England, however, they raided and conquered many of the areas around York; on November 1, 866, they captured the town itself. It soon rose to become the capital city of the Danelaw and the most important Viking town in England. York became a very large city, covering more than a hundred acres of land, and it was a great center of commerce and trade. About the year 1,000, a medieval writer described York as a,

> metropolitan city . . . nobly built and surrounded by firm walls yet now become old with age, although still enjoying a large population, numbering now more than 30,000 adults, a city amplified and greatly enriched by the wealth of merchants, who come from everywhere but especially from the Danish [Viking] people.[31]

Historians have always understood the importance of York to the Viking civilization, but it was not until the late twentieth century that any large-scale archaeological excavations were attempted. In the 1970s, archaeologists conducted an extensive dig in the center of the modern city of York. They found a rich treasure trove of Viking artifacts, proving that York had been a vibrant, important city. They also uncovered dozens of manufacturing areas that made such things as textiles, shoes, leather goods, and metalwork. The presence in York of many foreign goods, such as silk and wine jars, show a strong international trading community. Many Viking-era structures were

Pictured is one of the many Viking-era structures that have been uncovered in York, England.

also unearthed, showing how the Vikings of York lived and worked. The marvelous finds at York shed a great deal of light on the daily lives of ordinary, town-dwelling Vikings who lived there.

Settling Ireland

The settlement process was much different for Vikings in Ireland. They did not have a powerful Irish king or a mighty national army to contend with; they never faced a unified force that could defeat them. Thus, their attempts to establish themselves in Ireland went more smoothly and more easily than those in other parts of Europe.

When the Vikings began wintering in Ireland, they also began building permanent bases from which they could continue their raiding. In 841, for example, they built the first longport (a protected commercial center where the Vikings kept ships before a raid) in the area of Louth. They also constructed a longport in an area called Duib-linn, which means black pool. This longport grew to become the famous Irish town of Dublin. The Vikings went on to establish bases in other areas, such as *Hlymreir* (Limerick), *Veigsfjorth* (Wexford), *Vethrafjohr* (Waterford), and *Vikingalo* (Wicklow). These permanent Viking bases eventually became Ireland's first large-scale towns.

The Rise of Towns

The rise of Viking towns had a tremendous impact in both England and Ireland. Before the rise of these towns, agriculture was the main economic base. People lived from the products of individual farms, and traded for the few goods they could not grow or make. Wealth, then, was measured in crops and livestock.

Towns, however, created a central location where people, goods, and services could be found. As towns appeared, agriculture was not the culture's main economic base. Instead, most of the resources began to flow into urban areas where people gathered. Many people abandoned their farms for life in town, where they might find greater wealth and opportunity. Wealth was no longer measured in cattle and crops; goods and services became the benchmark of profit and prosperity.

Although the Vikings directly established some towns, they were more likely to influence the rise of urban areas indirectly. In the years when the Vikings terrorized the English and Irish coastlines, many ordinary citizens began to flee the rural, defenseless areas. The people then banded together in larger settlements for the first time in history. Some of these settlements rose in areas where there was a strong, stone church or monastery where the citizens might find safety during a raid. As more people emigrated to these areas, they began to establish their own trades and jobs within the settlement. Slowly, these areas turned into true towns.

Military leaders in England and Ireland also helped along the establishment of towns as they battled Viking invaders. Armies that fought the Vikings sometimes set up military camps and defensive structures in the countryside. Citizens who sought protection settled in these defensive areas, which soon became small towns.

Furthermore, trading settlements became towns in their own right. In some areas of the Danelaw, for example, settlements became centers of Viking trade.

Farming and Rural Life

Even though towns were on the rise, the Vikings were first and foremost an agricultural people, and their main goal in invading

TOWN VS. VILLAGE: WHAT MAKES A TOWN A TOWN?

In the years before the Vikings arrived in England, Ireland, and France, hundreds of small villages and settlements were scattered throughout the area. Some of these settlements, such as London and Paris, were large and prosperous.

A settlement or village is, according to most historians, a place where most of the inhabitants live off the resources of the surrounding area, creating many of the tools and objects they need for day-to-day life. A town, on the other hand, is different in that most people who live there have jobs other than that of farmer. They are traders, craftsmen, government officials, and other people who make their living by selling goods or services. People who live in a town must buy or trade for their food and other objects of daily life.

Before the Vikings, most English, Irish, and French settlements were little more than large agricultural areas where a few families grew crops. Some settlements where chieftains or kings lived might have been larger versions of these farming communities, but most of the inhabitants still lived off the surrounding landscape. When the Vikings arrived, they created longports, specific areas with a focused purpose: to provide a base for raiding and plundering the surrounding areas. Slowly these longports became centers for commerce, which attracted travelers, traders, and settlers. These people brought their own skills to the area, and eventually a town rose.

the areas they did was to find lands to farm. Because land represented power and wealth in their culture, the Vikings sought it with a passion.

Although historians have little evidence to reconstruct rural Viking life in England, Ireland, and France, most scholars agree that Vikings in these areas lived in much the same way they had in Scandinavia. Author Judith Jesch says,

Although some of the greatest achievements of the Viking Age are characterized by . . . wealthy and cosmopolitan trading centers, most people in fact still lived a rural life based on farming. This was true not only of the Danes, Norwegians and Swedes who stayed at home [in Scandinavia] but also of those who settled in . . . England or Normandy.[32]

The size of a Viking home varied, depending on the family's wealth or social status.

Viking life revolved around the homestead and farm. These varied in size, depending on the wealth of the family or their position in Viking society. They were usually isolated in the countryside, surrounded by the lands that the Viking family farmed for their livelihood. Most included a fenced-in area of land and buildings, but historians are unclear as to the purpose of many of the structures. They do know, however, that during the early Viking Age, many Viking families built a single structure to house themselves and their animals, which helped them to keep warm in the winter. Later on, though, many Vikings built separate structures for their farm animals.

A Viking farmer used whatever building materials he had on hand to construct his home. He might use clay, stone, or wood to build what he needed. Wealthy Viking nobles sometimes decorated their homes with intricate carvings and painted designs on the outside. Inside, Viking houses were usually divided into several rooms. The Vikings used firelight, candlelight, and the light from oil lamps inside their homes. They furnished their houses with rugs, wall hangings, tapestries, pillows, and cushions of cloth and fur. Many Viking women were accomplished weavers, and Viking homes usually had a loom standing in the corner of the main living area.

Most of what is known about Viking farming practices comes from archaeological excavations in Scandinavia, and historians speculate that settlers had similar practices in England and Ireland. In Scandinavia, Viking farmers usually grew such crops as barley, rye, oats, peas, beans, root vegetables, and cabbage. The fields often surrounded the house, as did the pastures where the Vikings kept their livestock. For many Vikings, their livestock herds were more important than their crops. Because there was little fertile land for farming in Scandinavia, many Vikings had become skilled herdsmen and livestock farmers. They kept cattle, pigs, and sheep, driving them up to higher pastures in the summer and bringing them back down to the farm in the fall and winter.

Because of the lack of fertile soil in Scandinavia, many Vikings valued their livestock above crops.

In their homelands, most Viking farmers lived in a particular area for about twenty years or so. By that time, they had exhausted the farmland and the nearby pastures. When this happened, they would move to a new area where the soil was better. Later, though, when the Vikings adopted Christianity, they began to build stone churches close to the best farmland and settle near these churches permanently.

Vikings as Traders

Although most Vikings did live on farms, some chose the faster pace of town life. These towns were usually centers of trade and commerce, not only for the Vikings but for everyone else who lived alongside them.

Early on, the Vikings used their extraordinary ships, sailing technology, and navigation skills to dominate the trade routes of Northern Europe. They sailed around the world, bringing goods to and from their Scandina-

BIRKA

In Scandinavia, the Vikings established and maintained a number of successful, rich market towns. Traders and merchants from around the world traveled there to buy and sell goods, bringing wealth to the local Vikings.

Birka was one of the most important merchant towns during the Viking Age. Situated on the small island of Bjorko in Lake Malar, it was at one time the largest town in Sweden. Historians are uncertain when the town was established, but know that it was in existence by the early 800s. During the Viking Age, visitors traveled to Birka and recorded what they saw there.

Historians know a lot about the trading at Birka due to the hundreds of graves that have been excavated. Most of the graves are filled with valuable goods such as coins, weapons, pottery, glass, and silk. These objects were imported from places as far away as Britain, Asia, and Russia, suggesting that Birka was a vibrant trading community.

The trading lasted until sometime in the middle of the tenth century. Then, for some inexplicable reason, Birka was abandoned. Today, historians have few clues to tell how and why such a rich town would have declined so quickly. One theory is that the water level of the lake fell, exposing land that blocked access to the sea. For whatever reason, though, by the late 900s Birka was a ghost town.

vian homelands. Scandinavia itself had strong markets with international reputations. Merchants and traders traveled north to acquire the riches that these markets offered.

As the Vikings began settling in other areas, they brought their markets and their trading styles with them, creating new trading opportunities in England, Ireland, and Europe. Historian Roesdahl says, "Trade flourished and the market grew with the Vikings' expansion in the North Atlantic, western Europe, and the British Isles."[33]

This trade relationship flourished because the different cultures had things the others wanted. Scandinavia had a seemingly inexhaustible amount of goods such as furs and amber that were highly prized in Europe. And the Vikings themselves wanted the goods from other cultures to the south of Scandinavia. As historian Gwyn Jones explains,

Always the north [the Vikings] needed gold and silver, ceramics and filigrees [a type of metalwork], glassware, fine fabrics, jewels and wine; and the south was greedy for the winter harvest of bearskins and sables, squirrel and marten [a fur-bearing animal], for walrus ivory and reindeer hides, wax and ship's cables, and always slaves, and a little amber.[34]

The Vikings saw their market towns as a vital part of their economy and power, and they were careful to establish their market areas in easily accessible places. Most were in good locations at the intersections of well-traveled roads, or perhaps in an area that could be accessed easily, such as near a beach or river where Viking ships could arrive and leave at will.

Although most historians refer to these Viking market areas as towns, they were not like modern towns, speculate historians Batey, Clarke, Page, and Price:

The towns founded by the Vikings in the eighth and ninth centuries were not like towns as we understand them today. They had no great public buildings built in stone, and we know little about how they were administered. They consisted of groups of wooden buildings, each containing a separate household with a dwelling-house and outbuildings within a fenced yard. Apart from the fact that the inhabitants gained their primary source of income from craft manufacture, there was little to distinguish their settlements from a village.[35]

Protecting the Towns

The Vikings understood the importance of their trading towns and the skilled craftspeople who lived in them. Thus they took great pains to protect them from invasion. The motivation was simple: market towns had to be safe places for people from around the world to buy and sell valuable goods, or no one would come to trade. In many cases, the local Viking chieftain made an official guarantee of peace and safety to those traveling to market towns. In return for this promise, the chieftain might receive some kind of payment, either in gold or in goods. In many cases, the kings or chieftains in Europe and Scandinavia would sign international agreements that kept their merchants safe in one another's lands. For example, in 873, the Viking King Sigfred of Denmark

VIKING JEWELRY

Vikings loved adorning themselves with gold, silver, and jewels. Both men and women wore jewelry, and many Viking graves include a variety of precious objects.

Men wore bracelets made of braided or twisted gold or silver. Many Viking stories, called sagas, relate the fact that kings or jarls usually gave such bracelets to their loyal followers in return for their service. Some men also wore a headbandlike object made of ribbons and gold. Historian Johannes Brondsted describes in his book *The Vikings* such an object that was found in the grave of a Viking warrior:

"[The warrior had] a couple of very finely made, streamer-shaped silk ribbons, the broad part of which showed delicate gold embroidery in an elaborate tendril pattern. These ribbons were probably the ornament called *hlad* in the sagas, which the Viking wore on his forehead. Even the toughest warriors enjoyed dressing in such finery."

Women had more jewelry than men, and they wore it with pride. They wore gold and silver twisted rings as necklaces or twined in their hair. Most women had large gold brooches, some called tortoiseshell brooches because they resemble the hollow shape of a tortoise shell, as well as other elegant brooches and pins. Women wore earrings as well. Both men and women wore armrings and necklaces made of precious glass beads imported from faraway lands.

This Viking brooch features intricate braiding and rich ornamentation. Both men and women wore jewelry.

and King Louis the German agreed, "to secure the peace in the lands between them . . .
so that the traders of both realms, when
they went over there [to Germany] and over
here [to Denmark] and brought wares with
them, should buy and sell in peace, all of
which the king for his part promised to
keep."[36]

For years, the Viking civilization thrived
and grew on the riches that trade and commerce brought. The Viking Age was a time
when great market centers rose and fell
throughout Europe. Vikings established trading towns in every area they invaded and settled, bringing new wealth and opportunity
with them.

CHAPTER FOUR

VIKING SOCIETY

The Vikings had a strong, vibrant culture that lasted for more than three hundred years, but we know little about how their society worked because they did not record their own history. They had no official accounts or records of their wars, kings, or the people who made up their civilization, and there is no clear reason to explain this. As a result, most of the information that historians have about Viking society comes from archaeological digs, accounts written by people who observed the Vikings during their own time, and from the rich legacy of Viking myths and sagas that were recorded after the Viking Age was over. By combining the information gleaned from these different sources, historians have been able to reconstruct a detailed picture of Viking society and how it worked.

Viking Class System

The Vikings had a very specific class society with three levels. Kings and nobles, or jarls, made up the highest class. According to historian Gwyn Jones, "[In this class] belonged the families with wealth, land, and rank. At different times during the Viking Age, and in different parts of Scandinavia . . . they enjoyed the rank of king or jarl over a defined territory."[37] Below them were the freemen, which included most of the Viking people. At the bottom of society were the slaves, or the unfree, as some accounts describe them.

This hierarchy of class determined how Vikings related to one another. The Vikings believed that each person was destined to live the life he or she was born into. This attitude was shared by all Vikings, regardless of where in Scandinavia or Europe they lived or what class they belonged to. Everyone had a special place in society, and each person played a vital role in the strength and growth of the Viking culture.

Kings and Nobles

Long before Vikings took to the sea and raided new lands, there were Viking kingdoms in Scandinavia, but historians are not clear about how big they were, what powers the kings or chieftains held, or how they ruled. However, some sagas and other written sources suggest that sometimes one king ruled over an area, or many jarls might have shared land and power at other times.

Kings were usually chosen for their political power and personal honor. However, it took more than honor to hold on to a kingship. The king's power derived from the honor and respect that other leaders gave him and was thus heavily dependent on the loyalty of the jarls in the kingdom. Historian Roesdahl says, "The individual regions retained their own customs and laws and a high degree of independence. The old aristocracy also had great power in the regions. . . . The

Long before Vikings took to the sea and raided other lands, there were Viking kingdoms in Scandinavia.

power of the king always depended on his interaction with the chieftains [jarls] and on international politics."[38]

Most of the time, the man who wanted to be king was a member of an old royal family, but that was not always the case. Sometimes, he was the son of a Viking noble, such as a wealthy landowner or prominent jarl. Although Viking kings came from the ruling class, the kingship itself was not necessarily hereditary. Usually, a king was succeeded by his son, but he did not have to be, and it was not always the oldest son who inherited the throne. Furthermore, in many cases, several members of one family would fight for the

throne. Most of the time, these disputing relatives reached an agreement, either dividing up the kingdom or deciding to rule together. In some cases, though, they went to war.

Regardless of a potential king's family or the results of an agreement, conflict, or war, he still had to be approved or elected by the people. According to historian Jones, "He [the king] depended . . . on the approval of his free subjects. His very election depended on their favorable voice at those public assemblies where he first presented himself to them. He had to carry them with him on all important decisions."[39]

In Sweden, for example, the king had to make a special tour, called a progress, throughout the country and present himself at the official Viking gatherings called Things. *Things* were regular meetings in which members of Viking society gathered to discuss laws and to vote on actions. One ancient Viking law says that, "The Swedes have the right to elect and likewise reject a king. . . . When he [the king] comes to the Thing he must swear to be faithful [to the people] . . . and he shall not break the true laws of our land."[40]

Characteristics of a King

Throughout Viking society, a king showed a number of characteristics that made him a powerful and respected person. He usually had a reputation as a strong fighter and a loyal person. This loyalty enabled him to convince men to follow him by the force of his personality.

A king was usually wealthy, and he could tempt potential followers with the promise of riches. Since most kings were descended from a line of aristocrats who commanded great wealth, they had control of much land and resources. Most of the profits from raids and wars

THE THING AND THE ALTHING

The Vikings were one of the first European societies to create a democratic form of government. They developed a public assembly of freemen that they called the Thing, the basis of Viking government throughout the Viking Age. Any Viking could bring a cause or a complaint before the Thing for members to vote on or to judge. The decision of the Thing was final, and most Vikings usually lived by what the Thing decided.

Most of the information that exists about the Thing comes from Iceland. There, the land was divided into four districts, and each district had its own Thing led by three *godar*, or leaders, in the area. Once a year, or at certain times of the year, all Vikings met at the grand Althing. Thirty-six *godar* controlled the Althing, and they elected a president, whom they called the Lawspeaker.

The Lawspeaker was one of the most important positions in Viking government, for he was the person who memorized all the laws that the Things and Althing followed. Because the Vikings did not write down their history or language, the Lawspeaker spent many months learning all the laws. He stayed in office for a renewable term of three years, and each year he was required to recite one-third of the entire Viking law. He had no authority to make decisions, but everyone turned to him for instructions on how to follow the law.

When the Vikings converted to Christianity, many of these laws were written down for the first time. But slowly, over time, the role of the king grew stronger, and the old Viking Thing faded.

The Viking Thing was one of the first examples of democratic government in Europe.

A great deal of a Viking king's prestige came from his ability to command ships and raid other lands for profit.

came in the form of land and treasure, and most of this went to the leader. He then used this wealth to reward loyal followers with money, goods, and land, which in turn created more loyalty among the powerful jarls. Freemen who went on raids with a king, for example, could expect such rewards, which created a strong bond of loyalty and trust between a king and his subjects.

In addition, a great deal of a king's prestige also came with his power to command ships and raid other lands for profit. Kings who con-trolled the sea-lanes in Scandinavia and else-where demanded payment from those who traveled them, and this in turn made other leaders respect his power and influence. As a result, he received loyalty and service from other influential traders and jarls.

Once a king was approved by the people, he still had to work hard to maintain their loyalty and trust. One way he did this was by trav-eling throughout the land to solidify loyalties and to recruit soldiers for his campaigns at home and raids abroad. He moved from one grand estate to the other throughout the land, with a large group of subjects and household members following along. They stayed at the farms of wealthy landowners as they traveled, and it was a great honor for a jarl to host the king and his attendants.

Financing the Kingship

Although a king was usually wealthy, maintaining all of his followers and paying his trusted advisors was a heavy financial burden. Most Viking kings did many things to increase their wealth throughout their reigns. Some of the king's wealth came from raids in foreign lands. The rich objects that the Vikings plundered from English and Irish monasteries, for instance, could be used to increase a king's treasury back home and to buy the loyalty of a large number of followers.

Kings also established trading centers and controlled the amount of goods that flowed through them. The king sometimes demanded tribute from merchants and others who came to buy and sell. He also agreed to protect those

VIKING WARRIOR WOMEN

Most of the contemporary accounts of the Vikings describe the savage and brave Viking men—tall, blond, and fierce. Few writers mention Viking women at all. Some evidence, however, suggests that men weren't the only ones who sought excitement and adventure beyond the walls of their homes. Viking women, too, were warriors and leaders in their own right.

One of the most telling accounts of female Viking warriors comes from a thirteenth-century work called the *History of the Danes*, written by a Christian clergyman named Saxo Grammaticus. He relied on old stories and legends from the Vikings' past to paint this picture, as Judith Jesch quotes in her book, *Women of the Viking Age*,

"There were once women in Denmark who dressed themselves to look like [men] and spent almost every minute cultivating soldiers' skills. . . . Loathing a dainty style of living, they would harden body and mind with toil and endurance, . . . compelling their womanish spirits to act with vile ruthlessness. . . . Those especially who had forceful personalities or were tall and elegant embarked on this way of life. . . . They put toughness before allure, aimed at conflicts instead of kisses, tasted blood, not lips, sought the class of [warrior's] arms rather than the arm's embrace, fitted to weapons hands which should have been weaving, desired not the couch but the kill, and those they could have appeased with looks they attacked with lances."

merchants and traders as they traveled in his lands—for another fee.

More wealth came from the king's large, self-sufficient farming estates. Viking kings usually owned a great deal of land, and they controlled a number of large farms that produced cattle and crops. A king could also increase his holdings by conquering a rival to the throne and then confiscating part of the loser's lands.

"Made for Honor, Not for Long Life"

But, for all the wealth and glory that many kings achieved, their power was fleeting, and they knew it. Since most Viking kings were also strong warriors, they continued to fight alongside their men in battle. As a result, many great Viking kings died young. For example, according to one saga, Norway's King Magnus Barefoot died when he was only thirty years old. Legend says he uttered a sentence that could have been a motto for all Viking rulers, "Kings are made for honor, not for long life."[41]

Furthermore, as the Vikings explored and settled in new lands throughout the early years of the Viking Age, the role of a king became less important. In the Viking settlement of Ireland, for example, the Vikings were content to have many smaller estates and areas controlled by local jarls. Historians suspect that the Viking spirit of individuality and independence was one cause of this. Vikings preferred to lead themselves rather than to let someone else govern them. Also, many of the Vikings who first raided and settled in lands outside Scandinavia were powerful leaders in their own right. They sought lands where they could maintain their own power and establish their own rules.

Freemen

Although the kings and jarls held the most political and economic power in Viking culture, they were not the ones who kept the civilization going throughout the Viking Age. It was the freemen who were the backbone of Viking society. They fought the battles, conducted the raids, settled the lands, and ultimately influenced the course of Viking expansion.

Most Vikings were part of this class. And the freemen, sometimes called peasants by historians, were primarily farmers. The Viking warriors who traveled the seas and raided faraway lands were also the same men who worked small farmsteads throughout Scandinavia and later, England, Ireland, France, Iceland, and Greenland. Jones says that, "The free man in possession of land and stock . . . was the backbone of a Scandinavia which, like the rest of Europe, was overwhelmingly pastoral and agrarian. Few . . . lived far or long from soil, seasons, crops, and beasts."[42]

Although freemen were primarily farmers, they sometimes held other professions. Some worked as farmhands and servants, plowing fields, hunting, and fishing. Others were merchants or professional warriors who followed a king or leader as he raided and pillaged foreign lands.

In some areas, Viking freemen were divided into different ranks. In Norway, for example, the higher rank of freemen owned inherited family land, while the lower rank farmed that land as tenants. There was also a third class of landless freemen, generally former slaves. Although the ownership of land gave some freemen more respect and honor than others, all freemen had similar rights under Viking law. They had the right to speak out at a Thing, and they voted on whether or not to approve their leaders.

THE *RIGSTHULA*

A famous Viking poem called the *Rigsthula* (Song of Rig), written sometime in the tenth century, vividly recounts the way the Vikings' different societal classes were created. Although the story is a myth, it illustrates how the Vikings perceived their way of life and how that way of life came to be.

According to the poem, Rig is the father of all mankind. One day, he came to the house of a poor couple named Ai and Edda. They fed him coarse, black bread, and Rig stayed with them for three days. Nine months after his visit, Edda gave birth to a son who was ugly, with lumpy knuckles and thick fingers. They called him Thrall. When he grew up, he married a woman named Slavey, and they had many children. Their boys were named Noisy, Roughneck, and Horsefly, and the girls had names like Lazybones, Beanpole, and Fatty. This family did all the hard labor such as carrying heavy loads, feeding the pigs, and cutting firewood. All slaves were descended from this family.

In the meantime, Rig had moved on and visited a second house. This home was much nicer than the first, and the couple inside were named Afi and Amma. They fed him, and he stayed three days. Nine months later, Amma had a son. He was strong and fresh with sparkling eyes. They called him Freeman. Eventually he married a pretty woman named Snor, and they had many children. They named the boys such things as Strongbeard, Husbandman, and Holder, while the girls had names like Prettyface, Maiden, and Capable. Freeman was responsible for taming oxen, building houses, and farming the land. Snor managed the house, took care of the money, and made meals and clothing for the family. All Viking freemen came from this family.

When Rig left this house he went to a wonderful, rich dwelling. In this hall he found another couple, Fadir and Modir. Once again, Rig stayed for three days, and nine months later, Modir had a beautiful blond son. He was strong and smart, and they named him Jarl (earl or warrior). He learned how to ride, hunt, and fight. Jarl went out into the world and made war, giving glory to himself. He gave treasure and land to his friends and followers. He married a beautiful woman named Lively, and they had many sons. One was named Kon (or king). These sons grew up to tame horses, fight with beautiful weapons, and learn the secrets of the sea. Viking kings and aristocrats were descended from Jarl and Lively.

Thus, freemen were an integral part of the civilization, and many researchers speculate that they led the expeditions across the sea, expanding Viking culture and seizing new lands. According to historian David M. Wilson,

[The freeman] class provided craftsmen and soldiers; some were peddlers, some may even have been merchants. They had protection under the law and played some part in its administration. It was probably from this class that many of the bands of Viking marauders [raiders] and traders were raised by the tough young aristocrats who financed the expeditions. The freemen who went on these expeditions would often have been the dissatisfied younger sons who saw no chance of bettering their position on the family's holding, and who had now a chance to win wealth and even land across the sea.[43]

Although the term *freemen* suggests that this class of Vikings was free to live in any way they pleased, the reality was that some of these people were only half-free. Although they were free to choose where to live and work, most freemen were still dependent on a more powerful Viking, a jarl or a king, for protection and wealth. For example, slaves who had purchased their freedom still owed loyalty and perhaps service to the person who had granted them freedom.

Slaves

But many slaves never became free and spent their lives in the control and service of their more powerful Viking masters. Slaves were at the lowest rung of Viking culture, and, because of this, little information exists about

how they lived and worked within society. The best sources of information come in the form of some Viking myths and sagas as well as laws that governed the treatment of slaves in England and Ireland. From this scattered evidence, it seems that the lives of slaves were full of hard labor. But they were also protected by law.

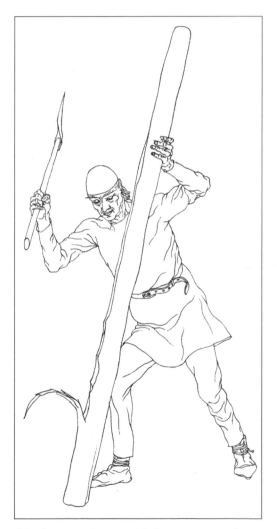

The freeman class provided carpenters and other craftsman that enabled the growth of Viking society.

A person could become a slave for many reasons. Someone condemned to death or charged with crimes might be sold into slavery, for example, and the children of slaves were automatically slaves when they were born. Occasionally, a family sold itself into slavery in a time of need. Most slaves, however, came from warfare. Some came from Viking areas where local jarls and kings battled one another and sold their prisoners into slavery. Others came from foreign countries, as historian Jones describes,

> [Slaves] came in great numbers from the British Isles, either caught in the dragnet of Viking raids and invasions or as straightforward objects of commerce; they came from all other countries where the Viking power reached; and above all they came from slave-hunts among the Slavonic peoples whose countries bordered on the Baltic [Sea].[44]

When the Viking raiders plundered the coasts of England and Ireland, they took many prisoners back to Scandinavia as slaves—men, women, children. Some they sold, and others they kept to work on their own farms. There is no information on exactly how many slaves lived in Scandinavia or the number of slaves in any individual household, but some Viking stories describe homes with dozens of slaves. Most historians, though, suspect that a profitable, well-to-do Viking farmer might have had only two or three slaves.

A Profitable Business

Slave trading was one of the most profitable aspects of Viking commerce. Vikings bought and sold slaves throughout Europe and Russia,

Pictured is a reconstructed Viking farm. Most large farms needed slaves to do the backbreaking labor necessary to keep them running.

and scholars suspect that at the height of the Viking Age the wealth brought by the slave trade was enormous. A successful raid, for example, could result in capturing a number of slaves, and the leader of the raid would be entitled to the profit gained by them.

Not only were slaves profitable as objects to sell, they were also the foundation of Viking life in Scandinavia. Large farms needed slaves to work the land and do the backbreaking manual labor that kept the farms running. Because of this, the Vikings considered slaves to be on the same level of importance as farm animals, although a slave was considered superior to a cow or horse. In England, for example, if a Viking's slave were killed—perhaps in anger or by accident—the killer had to pay the owner the worth of eight cows. In Ireland, the law said the killer had to pay eight ounces of silver.

Life as a Slave

One of the most gruesome aspects of a slave's life was the practice of sacrifice. Although historians debate how prevalent sacrifice was in Viking society, some evidence suggests that it was common practice to sacrifice slaves when their owners died. A few Viking burials have been found containing two bodies; scholars suspect that one was the body of a slave or servant. And during the tenth century, an Arab diplomat named Ibn Fadlan described a Viking funeral in which the dead man's slave was sacrificed and placed with him in the grave.

Despite the prospect of becoming a sacrifice, a slave's life in the Viking Age was not completely full of despair. Most Vikings treated their slaves well, and some evidence suggests that most slaves accepted their lot in life and tried to make the best of it. Mistreatment of slaves was considered to be as bad, if not

worse, than mistreatment of animals, and most Viking farmers took pains to treat their slaves kindly. Most slaves were allowed to own possessions, to marry and have children (although their children would be slaves), and most Viking lords allowed slaves time of their own to work for themselves.

Slaves could also work to buy their freedom, and it was common for a Viking to free a slave as a reward for good service. An example of this practice is illustrated in this description of one Viking farmer named Erling, written in the early eleventh century:

> Erling always had thirty slaves at home on his farm, besides other servants. He would allot the day's work to his slaves, but after this would give them their time free, with permission to every man who so wished to work for himself in the evening and at night. He gave them ploughlands to sow corn for themselves and let them use the crop for their own profit. He would assign a particular amount of work to each, to win himself freedom by doing it; and there were many who earned their freedom in this way in one year, or in the second year, and all who had any capacity for work could make themselves free within three years. With this money [Erling] bought other slaves. He taught some of his freed men how to work at herring fishing, and taught a useful craft to others, and some cleared fresh land for him, or built houses. Thus he helped the prosperity of them all.[45]

In this way, many slaves managed to gain their freedom, and freed slaves were

THE *HAVAMAL*

Viking society was bound by honor and loyalty to one's family, kin, and the gods. Those who broke the codes of honor faced losing their good reputations and the respect of the people. The Vikings had many rules of conduct that illustrate how important honor and loyalty were in their culture.

A celebrated Viking poem called the *Havamal* (The Sayings of the High One) describes some of the basic rules of conduct that most Vikings were expected to follow. Historian Else Roesdahl quotes these in her book, *The Vikings,*

"The tactful guest
will take his leave
early, not linger long
he starts to stink
who outstays his welcome
in a hall that is not his own.

The man who stands
at a strange threshold
should be cautious
before he cross it,
glance this way and that;
who knows beforehand
what foe may sit
awaiting him in the hall?

Cattle die,
kindred die,
every man is mortal,
but the good name
never dies
of one who has done well."

considered part of the freeman class. However, many of them still relied heavily on their former owners for protection and employment. These former slaves continued to farm a piece of the owner's land, paying rent in crops or money each year. Other former slaves, realizing that their futures were bleak without land and wealth, chose to follow a Viking leader in war or raids. Some chose to leave Scandinavia altogether, settling in England, Ireland, or in the faraway colonies of Iceland or Greenland.

All members of society, whether they were high-ranking Viking lords or the lowest slaves, had their place. Each played a vital role in the civilization, and all of them contributed in some way to the glorious time that was the Viking Age.

CHAPTER FIVE

RELIGION AND SPIRITUAL BELIEFS

Throughout most of the Viking Age, the Vikings believed in a complex religion filled with many gods and spirits who reflected the culture's attitude about honor and glory. The Christians who came in contact with the Vikings during this time, however, did not recognize that and called the Vikings *paganos*, which eventually became the word *pagan*—a derogatory term that the Christians used for anyone outside the Christian religion. Many Viking Age accounts describe the Vikings' pagan beliefs, which were eventually erased when Christianity spread throughout the Viking culture.

Information on Viking Religion Is Sketchy

Because the Vikings did not leave any written records describing their religion, researchers have very little information about Viking spiritual beliefs or religious practices. Instead, historians must rely on indirect evidence to piece together a picture of what the Vikings' religion must have been like.

Scholars can use as evidence descriptions left by the Christians who came in contact with the Vikings. However, although these firsthand accounts can relate a few details about Viking beliefs, historians cannot rely on them completely. Descriptions such as these are most likely biased because the Christians did not approve of the Viking religion. As a result, historians dismiss many details in these accounts as attempts by Christians to make the Vikings appear in the worst possible light.

Another source of information are the many Viking stories, or sagas, that were written down long after the Viking Age ended. The sagas recount lively stories of Viking deities and their exploits but give few hints about how these gods were worshipped from day to day. Some historians also look to modern Scandinavian fairy tales, superstition, and folklore for clues about ancient Viking beliefs. They speculate that modern folk rituals and beliefs, passed down for centuries, could provide clues to the ways the Vikings worshipped long ago.

Finally, archaeology has given scholars more information in the form of a few artifacts and objects that might have had religious significance to the Vikings. However, it is difficult for modern-day scholars to speculate about the religious significance of inanimate objects, and they are rarely able to offer an understanding of the Vikings' beliefs based solely on such evidence.

A VIKING MYTH

The Vikings believed in a colorful group of gods and goddesses. Many of the stories show the gods as having a mix of human and divine characteristics, making them seem both approachable and terrifying at the same time. They could also get into a lot of trouble. One humorous Viking tale relates the story of how the god Thor's hammer was stolen and how he got it back.

The story begins one day when Thor realizes his hammer is missing. He calls to Loki, another god, for help in finding it. Loki searches in the land of the jotuns, or giants, for Thor's magical hammer. He discovers that a jotun named Thrym stole it, and he will give it back only if the beautiful Viking goddess Freya agrees to marry him. Freya refuses, so Loki and Thor come up with a devious plan to steal Thor's hammer away from the jotun. They agree to dress Thor in a beautiful gown, cover his face with a veil, and present him to Thrym as Freya. Loki will go along, dressed as Frey's maid. According to the book *Norse Gods and Giants* by Ingri and Edgar D'Aulaire, the climax of the story occurs when the disguised Thor and Loki are sitting at the grand wedding feast that Thrym has prepared for himself and his "bride."

"Right away the bride [Thor] ate all the sweets on the table, then she devoured eight salmon and a whole roasted steer.

'My, I have never seen a bride eat so much!' Thrym exclaimed.

'The poor girl has had nothing to eat for eight days, she had pined away in her love for you,' Loki replied.

'Then let us begin the ceremony,' Thrym said. 'Bring Thor's hammer and put it in Freya's lap, and we shall make our marriage vows on it.'

Thor's heart laughed when the hammer was placed on his lap. He grabbed the handle and jumped to his feet. The veil fell off as Thor lifted the hammer and threw it across the room. Every jotun was smashed to bits by the great hammer.

Then Thor and Loki jumped into a cart and rode back to Asgard. Thunder rumbled and lightning flashed, and everyone in Asgard was happy once again."

Viking Attitudes About Life Influence Religion

Regardless, historians do know some things. For example, the men and women of the Viking Age lived in a land filled with harsh climate, unpredictable weather, mysterious forests, wild animals, impassable mountains, and other imposing aspects of the natural world. They believed that this natural world was controlled by the powerful forces of the gods. They also believed that evil forces in the form of storms, hail, disease, and snow were at work to destroy their people. The Vikings believed that they had to struggle against these forces to ensure the future of their people so that the crops might grow and so that their children might have a pleasant place to live. They also believed it was inevitable that they would have to fight the forces trying to destroy them.

However, they did not struggle against the forces alone. The Vikings believed in the strength and power of their families and their tribes. To them, each member of the group had a responsibility to the others, and each person was expected to give help when it was needed. From this basic belief arose the idea of loyalty and honor to one another. Thus, a man who was known as a loyal and honorable per-

Vikings held the belief that evil forces in the form of storms, hail, disease, snow, and other natural phenomenon were constantly at work to destroy their people.

son could command a great deal of power in the group. A man's reputation as an honest and honorable person reflected on his entire family, and a good reputation could ensure that his family's name lived on after they were dead. Historian Edvard Henriksen explains this Viking idea of honor, saying,

> Honor expresses a man's investment, the fullness of his life. Life itself is expressed in honor, and it is a matter of honor to hold one's own, especially against insult and injustice, and this is the same for the individual as for the family. . . . Life and honor must be maintained, now and in the future, or the individual and the family will sink into nothingness. The struggle is never-ending, forever demanding alertness and vigilance.[46]

This idea of honor and strength translated directly into the Vikings' spiritual beliefs and their attitudes toward their gods. The gods could not change or alter the course of the world; everything that happened was destined to occur. As a result, the Vikings believed it was how one faced adversity that mattered. Fighting the good fight with honor and skill was the most important thing any Viking could do.

Their gods epitomized this idea of honor and strength against adversity. The gods were immortal, but they were also living, breathing entities whom the people could call on for help, just as they could call on their family and their neighbors in times of trouble. The Vikings believed that their gods would come to their aid in times of need, just as their friends and family would. So rather than worship the gods as lofty deities, the Vikings perceived their

gods as partners of sorts, to be asked for assistance when the need arose. According to Henriksen, "The Scandinavian [Viking] does not piously submit to the will of the gods; he wills, and men and gods must join him in this willing. . . . Just as there was help to be had in the struggle from family and fellow tribesmen . . . so also from divine powers."[47]

The Viking sagas describe gods who epitomized all that the Vikings aspired to be: honorable, trustworthy, powerful, strong, and wise. They respected family and honored their comrades. They also, like the Vikings themselves, understood the futility and inevitability of life and death. Writer Kevin Crossley-Holland says,

> The gods are heroic figures . . . who led dangerous, individualistic lives, yet at the same time were part of a closely-knit small group, with a firm sense of values and certain intense loyalties. They would give up their lives rather than surrender these values, but they would fight on as long as they could, since life was well worthwhile. Men knew that the gods whom they served could not give them freedom from danger and calamity, and they did not demand that they should. We [people today] find in the myths no sense of bitterness at the harshness and unfairness of life, but rather a spirit of heroic resignation: humanity is born to trouble, but courage, adventure, and the wonders of life are matters of thankfulness, to be enjoyed while life is still granted to us. The great gifts of the gods were readiness to face the world as it was, the luck that sustains men in tight places, and the opportunity to

win that glory which alone can outlive death.[48]

Viking Gods and Goddesses

Historians believe that the Vikings worshipped hundreds of gods, and while many people may have worshipped the major gods, not everyone worshipped all deities. Each local village or tribe likely had its own set of gods and goddesses. Very little information remains about most of these gods, except for a few place-names scattered throughout Scandinavia and Europe suggesting a particular god was worshipped there. For example, the Norwegian island of Tysnesoen was once known as Njaroarlog, which translates to bath of Njord. Njord was the Viking god of the sea, and historians believe that this

IBN FADLAN

Of all the written accounts of the Vikings, the most famous one was recorded by Ibn Fadlan, a Muslim diplomat. He traveled with a group of Vikings, called Rus, in 922, and his manuscript is the earliest known eyewitness account of Viking life. Today, many historians consider Ibn Fadlan's account to be one of the most accurate pictures of life during the Viking Age.

Very little is known about Ibn Fadlan or his life. He was an educated, eloquent man who was part of the court of the caliph (king) of Baghdad. He was originally sent as an ambassador to the king of the Bulgars, which was a group in Russia at the time. However, during Ibn Fadlan's journey he fell in with a band of Vikings and ended up adventuring with them instead. He was gone for three years; when he returned, he dutifully recorded his adventures in the form of a report to the court. Although his original manuscript is lost, numerous copies have been found around the world. Together, they tell an amazing story of Vikings in the tenth century.

One of Ibn Fadlan's descriptions is quoted in *The Vikings* by Johannes Brondsted,

"I saw the Rus when they arrived on their trading mission. . . . Never have I seen people of more perfect physique; they are tall as date-palms [a tree], and reddish in color. They wear neither coat nor mantle [overgarment], but each man carries a cape which covers one half of his body, leaving one hand free. Each man has [tattooed upon him] trees, figures, and the like, from fingernails to the neck."

name suggests that this island was once sacred to that god.

Almost all the information we have about Viking gods comes from poetry and stories written during the thirteenth century, long after the Viking culture disappeared. These written sources suggest that the Viking gods were divided into two major families, the Aesir and the Vanir.

Odin

The Aesir was the larger family of Viking gods, whose head god was Odin, the god of power and wisdom. Odin is often referred to as the Allfather in Viking mythology. This term meant two things to the Vikings: Odin was the father of all the other gods and goddesses, and he was also the first and greatest of them. A thirteenth-century Icelandic writer named Snorri Sturluson described Odin, saying, "Odin . . . rules all things and, no matter how mighty the other gods may be, they all serve him as children do their father. . . . He lives for ever and ever, and rules over the whole of his kingdom and governs all things great and small. He created heaven and earth and sky and all that in them is."[49]

The Vikings considered Odin to be the god of battle, warriors, and kings. His home was a great long hall called Valhalla. They believed that specially chosen Viking warriors killed in battle would be taken to Valhalla by the Valkyries, a group of battle maidens. There, the dead would feast and drink, celebrating their honor and glory in battle. The Vikings considered it to be a

In addition to being the chief Norse god, Odin was also the god of battle, poetry, and wisdom.

great honor to die and be delivered to Odin in Valhalla.

Not only was Odin the god of battle, he was also the god of poetry and wisdom. According to Viking myths, Odin has a thirst for learning. In one myth, for example, he sacrifices an eye in exchange for knowledge, and in another he voluntarily hangs himself for nine days in order to learn magical secrets.

Most Viking gods owned many magical objects, and Odin was no exception. He rode on a magical eight-legged horse called Sleipnir. His magic spear was called Gungnir, and he also owned a magical ring called Draupni. One of Odin's most remarkable possessions, though, was a magical seat called Lidskjalf. When he sat there, he could see everything that happened in the mortal world and in the world of the gods. On each shoulder perched two huge ravens, Huginn (thought) and Muninn (memory). As two storytellers recounted,

> When Odin sat on Lidskjalf, two . . . black ravens perched on his shoulders. At dawn he would send the ravens off to fly over the world and look into the darkest corners. At noontime they would come back to sit on his shoulders and whisper into his ears all the secret things they had learned. Nothing was hidden from Odin . . . when he sat on Lidskjalf.[50]

Odin was a powerful god, but he was not well loved. Instead, the sagas suggest that he was greatly feared because he would stop at nothing to achieve his goals. Odin was, to the Vikings, like a powerful ally whose strength they respected but whom they could not trust completely. According to Johannes Brondsted, "To achieve his aim of gaining all wisdom and knowledge of all mysteries Odin stops at nothing in the way of deceit, cunning, and treachery."[51]

Thor

If Odin was the greatest of the Viking gods, Thor, his son, was the best loved. While Odin represented violence and war, Thor represented order and stability. Writer Kevin Crossley-Holland says, "It is clear from the terms in which [Thor] is described by . . . the saga writers, and from the large number of place-names embodying his

name, that he was the most loved and respected of the gods."[52]

Thor was the god of the freemen. Many Viking sagas and stories depict him as the strong and loyal protector of the people. Viking farmers thought of him as a helpful god who made crops grow; in some areas he was the god of agriculture. Because the Vikings saw Thor as such an important part of daily life, he seemed more real to them than any of the other gods.

Throughout Viking myths, Thor is the god who is honest, kind, and unfailingly

The best loved of all the Norse gods, Thor was seen as the god who helped and protected the people.

mitt. Thor also owned a magic belt that, according to Viking myth, doubled his strength when he wore it. When he wore the belt and wielded Mjolnir, Thor was almost invincible.

Thor also drove a magical chariot pulled by a team of goats. The Vikings believed that the sound of thunder during a storm was the rumble of Thor's chariot wheels as they rolled across the sky.

Njord, Frey, and Freya

The other family of Viking deities was called the Vanir. According to legend, the Vanir were a much older race of gods than the Aesir. The two families of gods fought often but finally made peace and exchanged hostages. Njord, Frey, and Freya were the three Vanir gods who went to live with the Aesir.

Njord was the god of the sea. He ruled the ocean during storms, and many Viking seafarers prayed to him. He was also the god of sea travel, trade, and wealth, all very important aspects of life during the Viking Age. According to myth, Njord was so important that the gods of the Aesir gave him his own sparkling hall with a grand shipyard at the shores of the seas of the world.

Njord's son, Frey, also called the god of plenty, was the most important fertility god to the Vikings, and archaeologists have found many objects depicting him. The great number of these objects suggests that Frey was widely worshipped throughout Viking lands. Snorri Sturluson wrote, "Frey is an exceedingly famous god; he decides when the sun shall shine or the rain come down, and along with that the fruitfulness of the earth, and he is good to invoke for peace and plenty. He also brings about the prosperity of men."[54]

Frey's sister, Freya, was much like her brother, according to Viking myth. She, too,

This Viking amulet, or religious charm, includes a representation of Thor's hammer, Mjolnir.

loyal. Even his physical description suggests someone any man would be proud to call kin. According to Crossley-Holland, "[Thor's] physical image fits the role well; he was huge, red-bearded, possessed of a vast appetite, quick to lose his temper and quick to regain it, a bit slow on the uptake, but immensely strong and dependable."[53]

Like Odin, Thor also possessed magical objects. His greatest was a mighty hammer called Mjolnir. It was said that Mjolnir smashed everything it struck. Thor also had a magical iron mitt. When he flung Mjolnir at an enemy, it would kill its target and fly back to Thor's hand. Although the hammer was red hot, Thor could catch it safely with his iron

was a deity of fertility and growth, as well as the goddess of love and beauty. Freya was the most beautiful of the Viking goddesses, beloved by men and women alike. But according to the Viking sagas, she was also associated with war and battle. She rode into battle in a grand chariot pulled by cats, and some Viking sagas explain that Freya divided the slain warriors of the battlefield with Odin; half went to Valhalla, and half went to her hall called Sessrumnir.

Like the other deities, Freya had many magical possessions. She was, in fact, the goddess of magic and owned a falcon skin that enabled her to take the form of that bird. Freya would put on the falcon skin, then fly throughout the world, bringing back knowledge of the future.

Loki

Loki is at once one of the most charming and dangerous of the Viking gods. Although, according to Viking myth, Loki was the son of giants, Odin chose him as a blood brother and invited him to live with the gods. Loki figures into many Viking myths as a cunning and deceitful trickster who causes great mischief and harm in the Viking world. One author described Loki as, "handsome and fair of face, but [he] has an evil disposition and is very changeable of mood. He excelled all men in the art of cunning, and he always cheats. He was continually involving the Aesir in great difficulties and he often helped them out again by guile [trickery]."[55]

It is doubtful that any Vikings actually worshipped Loki. Instead, Loki was the example of chaos and uncertainty in the world, a dishonest and cruel god who caused much pain and sadness. To the Vikings, Loki must

have represented the hardships they had to face in their everyday lives. According to Brondsted, "Loki . . . has no sense of humor. He is cunning and deceitful and lacks all capacity for friendship; his stinging words can hurt and strike, and his attacks on practically all the gods and goddesses are invariably vicious and cruel."[56]

Loki, like the rest of the gods, had his own personality, complete with very human strengths and weaknesses. The Vikings identified with these attributes, which made the gods seem real to them. As a result, the Vikings believed that they had a chance to ascend to the place of the gods and celebrate with them in their grand, eternal halls when they died. Their burial customs, according to historians, reflected this belief.

Viking Burials

Archaeologists look at Viking burials for information about religious beliefs and customs, and much of what they have discovered points to a complex and rich belief system. The basis of this system, historians suspect, is the respect and loyalty of the family and kin of the departed person. However, the burial sites are so different from one another that it is difficult to pin down exactly what the Vikings believed about the dead and the afterlife. Brondsted explains this: "The Viking attitude towards death is to some degree disclosed through grave finds. Hundreds of Viking graves have been unearthed. . . . But, far from presenting a uniform impression of the Viking idea of the afterlife, they reveal a great complexity and variety of practice and belief."[57]

Part of the vast difference in Viking burials has to do with location. It appears

VIKING RUNES

Although the Vikings did not record their own history, they did have a type of lettering called runes. The runic alphabet is called the futhark, from its first six characters. Runes were developed, according to many historians, as a way to incise letters on hard objects such as bone, wood, and stone. They consist of a series of lines drawn in different configurations that could be easily scratched into a hard surface. Archaeologists have found runes carved on hundreds of Viking objects, such as ships, weaving implements, combs, and brooches. Most of these runes spell only the owner's name, but some may have been a sort of magical inscription.

So many runic inscriptions exist that historians suspect many Vikings were literate. Scandinavia is dotted with large monuments carved with runes, called rune stones, that give the barest of clues as to the lives of the men and women who made them. Most of them are memorial stones, erected by friends and family members who wanted to record the names and deeds of their loved ones in runes for all time.

Viking lettering, or runes, are seen here carved into a stone found in Sweden.

that there were two different burial customs in the various areas of Denmark, Norway, and Sweden: burial and cremation. Many historians think this is due to a difference in religious beliefs, while others suggest that it was caused by a number of factors, including local customs, wealth, social status, and the influence of Christianity.

Although historians do not know exactly why the Vikings practiced these rites, they believe it has to do with the Vikings' two different ideas of the afterlife. One idea is that the dead continue to live in their graves as they would in a home, which meant that they had to be buried with all the things they needed in order to continue. The other belief was that the dead had to be sent forth on their journey to the otherworld.

These ideas can be seen in Viking myth and sagas as well. Many stories tell of the dead living in their burial mounds or in a holy mountain, surrounded by treasures and weapons. Others mention the distant lands of the gods, such as Valhalla, and the dark underworld controlled by the goddess Hel, which was the destination of the wicked. These stories, according to scholars, reinforce the idea that the Vikings had different death beliefs and practiced burial customs that reflected these beliefs.

Burials

Not only did religion figure into the Vikings' burial beliefs, but the idea of a strong, loyal family also played a part. It was the family, says Brondsted,

> which built and preserved the grave, mound, or cemetery, however the dead were disposed of. Here the fam-

ily kept its dead, and here in a sense they lived on, even if they visited Valhalla or Heaven in between. Or the dead might live on within a holy mountain or hill near the ancestral farm. The dead were always with the family, and for that reason it was a family obligation always to maintain the grave or the burial mound in good order.[58]

In most burials, the body was laid directly on the ground, sometimes covered with a cloak. Sometimes pillows would be laid beneath the body. A man would be surrounded by his weapons and tools; a woman would have her jewelry and her tools, perhaps her loom or cooking utensils, as well. Many of these graves would then be covered with an earthen mound or surrounded by stones set in a circle, square, or even the shape of a ship. In some parts of Scandinavia, a strong wooden chamber was also built to house the dead. An Arab by the name of Ibn Rustah witnessed such a burial and described it, saying, "When a great man among them [the Vikings] dies, they make a grave like a large house and place him in it. With him they lay his clothes, the gold arm-rings he wore, and also much food, and bowls of drink, and coins."[59]

The most elaborate and famous types of burials, however, were Viking ship burials. In some cases, a wealthy or important person was laid inside a full-sized Viking ship filled with goods and treasure. The ship was then buried beneath a huge earthen mound. In many cases, animals such as dogs and horses would be sacrificed and laid with the corpse as well. Sometimes a human, perhaps a slave or a beloved spouse, was sacrificed and laid alongside the dead. Much of the information that historians have discovered about the Viking Age comes from such burials and the objects found inside them. Jacqueline Simpson describes some of these burials, located in the Scandinavian areas of Vendel and Valsgarde,

Here, generation after generation, the head of the family was interred in exactly the same manner—sitting or lying in the ship's stern, facing a pile of goods heaped in the bow, and with his weapons by his side or actually in his grasp; slaughtered horses and dogs were

In most Viking burials, the body was laid directly on the ground, covered with a cloak, and surrounded by weapons, tools, and other items a person would need in the afterlife.

Among the Vikings, the most elaborate and famous types of burials were ship burials.

lined up in pairs inside or outside the ship.[60]

Cremation

The other major funeral tradition of the Vikings was cremation. This type of death rite, according to the medieval historian Sturluson, was a hallmark of warrior Vikings who worshipped Odin. He explains,

> Odin made it a law that all dead men should be burnt, and their belongings laid with them on the pyre [flames], and the ashes cast into the sea or buried in the ground. He said that in this way every man would come to Valhalla with whatever riches had

been laid with him on the pyre. . . . It was their [the Vikings'] belief that the higher the smoke rose in the air, the higher would be raised the man whose pyre it was, and the more goods burnt with him, the richer he would be.[61]

Archaeologists have found cremation sites throughout Scandinavia, and the widespread evidence of cremation suggests to historians that it was a common practice throughout Viking lands. In most cases, the burning took place in one area, then the ashes would be moved to their final resting place. Once the large funeral pyre had died down, friends and family took the charred remains and spread them on the chosen area. Larger items, such as weapons, might be deliberately damaged and then piled on top of the ashes, although archaeologists are uncertain why this particular ritual was followed. Finally, the pile would be buried beneath a mound of earth, and sometimes a memorial stone would be placed on top of the mound.

The Vikings also participated in cremation ceremonies, the most famous type of which was that of the burning ship. According to some historians, the corpses of rich or important Vikings were sometimes placed on a ship, which was then set on fire and floated out to sea. Although some ancient accounts describe such a burial, few other records exist to suggest that ship burning was commonly practiced. As a result, most scholars believe it was a rare event.

Regardless of the type of funeral a person had, all Vikings had burial rituals. Families and friends always prepared the dead for their passage into the next life, and burial mounds were carefully maintained for beloved family members. Thus, the Vikings honored their deities and their fallen loved ones in death as in life, with respect and loyalty.

CHAPTER SIX

THE GOLDEN AGE OF VIKING EXPLORATION

During the Viking Age, the Vikings burst from Norway, Denmark, and Sweden to attack, then to settle, in many new areas. Although the Vikings are well known for their raids and settlements in England, Ireland, and France, it was their more distant adventures into the areas of modern-day Russia, Greenland, Iceland, and even North America that had the greatest impact.

Vikings in Russia

During the early days of the Viking Age, when marauding groups of warriors plundered the coasts of England and Ireland, other Vikings were exploring different areas of the world. Those who lived in Sweden, for example, struck out from their homelands and sailed east, toward the Baltic region and lands that encompass modern-day Russia.

Although no written accounts of the Vikings' earliest forays into Russia exist and the archaeological evidence of their presence is sketchy at best, there have been enough archaeological finds to enable researchers to form some opinions about Swedish Vikings in Russia. Viking graves, for example, have been found in the Russian areas of Latvia and Gdansk.

Most historians agree that the Vikings did not go to Russia to raid or to settle the lands, as those in England and Ireland did. The Vikings who explored Russia wanted to trade. Historian Brondsted explains, "The Swedes did not penetrate Russia with the intention of conquest and settlement, as the Danes did in England and France; they set out to establish and maintain extensive trade-routes."[62]

It was only a short journey from Sweden across the Baltic Sea and into Russia. Many large rivers flow into the Baltic, and the Vikings used them as convenient freeways to sail inland. There were also trading centers already set up around the mouths of some of these Russian rivers. Historian Roesdahl explains,

> Some rivers led to trading centers such as Staraja Ladoga near the Gulf of Finland . . . Novgorod near the Volchov [River]'s source in Lake Ilmen; Kiev on the Dnieper [River], and Bulgar on the bend in the Volga where the Volga and the Kama [Rivers] merge. Along these waterways the Scandinavians moved freely.[63]

The Vikings who traveled inland on these rivers found a variety of cultures that were ready and willing to trade with them. West Slav tribes, for instance, lived south of the

Baltic Sea, while a people known as the Finno-Ugric made their homes in the east, along the Volga River and up the coast to the Gulf of Finland. The Vikings also came in contact with a people known as the Bulgars and Khazars, as well as many other smaller groups. To the Swedish Vikings, these new areas were filled with an abundance of wealth, and they wanted a part of it.

Establishing Viking Rule

The Vikings arrived in Russia sometime early in the ninth century, at about the same time that other Vikings were sending vast armies and settlers to England and Ireland. One of the most reliable accounts of the Vikings' arrival in Russia is included in an ancient document called *The Russian Primary Chronicle*, or *Nestor's Chronicle*. This document was compiled in about A.D. 1113 by a monk in the city of Kiev. The document refers to Vikings as "Varangians" and recounts how, in about A.D. 860, the Vikings first demanded money and goods, called a tribute, from the local tribes. The local tribes resented this and, according to the chronicle,

> The tributaries [locals] of the Varangians drove them back beyond the sea and, refusing them further tribute, set out to govern themselves. But there was no law amongst them, and tribe rose against tribe. . . . And they said to themselves, "Let us find a king to rule over us and make judgements according to the law." And they crossed the sea to the Varangians, to the Rus, for these Varangians were called Rus as others were called Swedes. . . . And to the Rus they said,

Many of the Viking trading ships that ventured east into Russia found numerous cultures willing to establish a trading relationship.

In order to facilitate trade, many Viking merchants adopted the customs and dress of the areas in which they conducted business.

"Our land is large and rich, but there is no order in it. So come and be king and rule over us."[64]

This was a significant event in that the local Russian people actively sought out the leadership of foreign Vikings to rule them.

The story continues by explaining that a Viking named Rurik settled in the town of Novgorod; another named Sineus went to the town of Beloozero; and, finally, Truvor settled in the town of Izborsk. The Vikings then swiftly took control of these three major trading centers and began to control the outlying areas.

The Russian Primary Chronicle mentions that in 880 another Viking, known only as Oleg, marched from Novgorod to Kiev with a great army and took control of the city. According to the chronicle, "Oleg set himself up as prince of Kiev, and declared that it should be the mother of Russian cities. . . . Oleg began to build stockade [protected] towns, and imposed tribute on neighboring tribes."[65]

Oleg's most significant achievement, historians suggest, was the fact that he set up trade relations with the Byzantine Empire, which was the most powerful culture in the world at the time. Based in the city of Constantinople, now known as Istanbul in Turkey, it was the center of trade and commerce throughout the world. Constantinople was also a glittering jewel of excitement, power, and wealth. According to historian Magnusson, "It was a memorably beautiful place, with innumerable domes and . . . towers all gleaming in the sun. . . . Constantinople was the mecca, the magnet, for every merchant and mercenary [soldier for hire] from every known corner of the world."[66]

An agreement with the leaders of Constantinople would guarantee unlimited waves of wealth for the Vikings, and Oleg set out to grab it in typical Viking fashion: He attacked the city. In the year 907, Oleg's huge fleet of ships swept down the Dnieper River from Kiev and across the Black Sea to Constantinople. According to legend, the defenders tried to stop the ships by stretching huge iron chains across the Bosporus River, but Oleg's warriors dragged their lightweight ships to shore and carried them around the blockade.

Rather than battle such a powerful army, the leaders of Constantinople agreed to a trading treaty. It gave Viking merchants many special privileges for such things as grain, bread, wine, meat, fish, and other supplies. The Vikings gained access to markets and gear for their ships and were exempt from taxes on the goods they sold. But the leaders of Constantinople did not trust the Vikings, for the treaty also stipulated that the only Vikings allowed in the city were merchants who were required to live outside the city and to enter through only one gate, and then only if they were unarmed.

This treaty opened up vast riches to Viking traders and merchants, and for many years Vikings came to Constantinople by the hundreds. Kiev became the gateway to Constantinople, and it grew to be a large and prosperous city in its own right.

Decline of the Vikings in Russia

Little is known, however, about the Vikings who lived in Russia and who probably found wealth and fame as traders in Constantinople, for they left almost no evidence behind in these areas. The Vikings did not found cities of their own; the towns they lived in had been

Pictured is the city of Constantinople. In 907, Oleg successfully set up trade relations with the Byzantine Empire.

settled by local tribes long before they arrived. Thus, there were no purely Viking settlements for archaeologists to discover and to study.

Since the Vikings left no written records, scholars must piece together the history from accounts, such as the *Russian Primary Chronicle*, that were written hundreds of years after the Viking Age ended. As a result, researchers have no concrete evidence as to why and how the Viking power in Russia eventually declined.

Historians strongly suspect, however, that one of the reasons for the Viking decline was their assimilation into the local culture. Russia had been populated by many groups, known collectively as Slavs. When Swedish Vikings arrived in Russia, they interacted with the Slavic cultures on a daily basis. In addition, the Vikings who traveled to Russia were mostly men looking for wealth and adventure. Many who stayed married local women, and their descendants adopted Slavic names and customs. These Vikings also began to learn the local language, leaving their Scandinavian language behind. Furthermore, many Vikings converted to Christianity during this time, which caused them to abandon their traditional ways. As a result, by the eleventh century, the Vikings who had stayed in Russia were part of the Slavic culture.

Vikings in Iceland and Greenland

Of all the great raids, settlements, and trading conquests that the Vikings enjoyed throughout the Viking Age, their greatest cultural achievement was the discovery and settlement of the areas of Iceland and Greenland. During the years that the Vikings settled these lands, especially Iceland, their culture saw its finest growth and strength. According to historian Logan,

The Viking civilization reached its highest point amidst the glaciers, ice, sandy beaches, lava plains and green meadows of Iceland. Nowhere else did the Vikings establish a sizeable permanent settlement of their own, undisturbed by native peoples, by the necessities of conquest, and by the consequent of absorption.[67]

Iceland is a large island northwest of Britain, near the Arctic Circle. It is a land of ice, glaciers, and active volcanoes. Although a few Christian monks knew about Iceland, it was the Vikings who made the first permanent settlements there. One famous medieval text known as *Landnamabok* (The Book of the Landtaking) credits three different Vikings with the discovery of Iceland. One was named Naddod, who accidently discovered the island sometime before the year 870, "[Naddod and his shipmates] were driven by a storm into the western ocean and found there a big country. . . . They stayed until autumn, and, as they left, they saw snow on the mountain tops and, thus, they called the land Snowland."[68]

The second was called Gardar. The *Landnamabok* says,

There was a man named Gardar Svarvarsson, by descent a Swede, who set off in search of Snowland. . . . He made landfall east of the Eastern Horn, where there was a harbor. Gardar circumnavigated the land and discovered it was an island. . . . In the spring Gardar returned to Norway and praised the land highly. The land was now called Gardarsholm.[69]

Finally, a third Viking named Floki Vilgerdarson set out for Gardarsholm, and the *Landnamabok* claims that when he and his men found it, they "took so much advantage of the excellent fishing there that they neglected to make hay, and all their livestock died during the winter. A rather cold spring followed. Floki climbed up a high mountain, faced north, and saw a fjord full of ice and called the land Iceland."[70]

Although some historians question the accuracy of these stories, they agree that Viking explorers had found Iceland sometime in the years before 870. For about sixty years, from 870 to 930, thousands of Viking immigrants sailed from Norway and Ireland to settle in Iceland.

The Vikings left their homeland in droves for many reasons. For some, Iceland was a place to find excitement and adventure. For others, it was a place where they could find land of their own to farm and to settle. One of Iceland's advantages was that it was uninhabited, so the Vikings who craved land did not have to fight people already living there to get it.

Additionally, political factors in Scandinavia at the time may have contributed to the mass immigration. Norway had recently been unified under King Harald Finehair. Historians suspect that many of the immigrants were enemies of the new king who decided to leave their homeland rather than submit to his rule.

EARLY ACCOUNTS OF ICELAND

Centuries before the Vikings settled in Iceland, some ancient historians had heard of a faraway, frozen land they called Thule. This land, according to old accounts, was about a six-day journey from Britain. In the later decades of the eighth century, a small group of Irish monks had traveled to this cold land and founded a tiny outpost where they worshipped. A description of the land where they lived, written by a geographer of the time, is reprinted in Historian F. Donald Logan's book, *The Vikings in History*, "Not only at the summer solstice [in June] but in the days round about it the sun setting in the evening hides itself behind a small hill in such a way that there was no darkness."

Although these ancient writings are vague, they describe Thule as a cold land that had the same characteristics as Iceland, including a sun that does not set in the summer, a common phenomenon in areas close to the Arctic Circle. Further, the Vikings who landed on Iceland recorded finding the remains of a small outpost, perhaps that of the eighth-century monks. Thus, modern historians suspect that Thule was indeed Iceland.

The Viking spirit of individualism and self-government may have also played a role. Historian Roesdahl explains,

> According to Icelandic literature, the desire for liberty was an important incentive [to immigrate]; many Norwegian chieftains departed in order to avoid subjection to King Harald Finehair. None of the . . . pioneer communities [in Iceland] had a king. . . . And they remained . . . with a certain democracy and a high degree of independence until long after the Viking Age.[71]

Regardless of the reasons, within a sixty-year period Iceland was populated by as many as thirty thousand Vikings. The first settlers brought everything they would need for a new life: cattle, household goods, foods, seeds to plant crops, and farming tools. Until their crops could grow, the people lived by hunting and fishing. Every year, news of the success of the settlements reached Scandinavia, and more boats full of hopeful immigrants arrived on Iceland's shores.

The Vikings brought their entire culture and belief system with them to Iceland. They governed the same way they did in Scandinavia, with assemblies called Things presided over by local chieftains and other freemen. The members of the Things decided laws and heard legal disputes, just as they had done in the homeland.

Most historians agree that Iceland was completely settled by about 930. By that time, all the good farmland had been taken; a vibrant society had been established; and the island was thriving with agriculture. But for some Vikings, the settled landscape was not enough. They longed to find new lands to explore.

Greenland

Greenland, about two hundred miles northwest of Iceland, is a huge, cold land with few habitable areas. It remained hidden to the Vikings until about 900, when a Viking named Gunnbjorn was blown off course during a voyage from Norway. According to historian Logan, "The first recorded sighting of Greenland took place about 900 and, as elsewhere, came from a storms-tossed, bearings-lost ship, this the ship of Gunnbjorn, on its way from Norway to Iceland. . . . Gunnbjorn, thrown off course to the south, sailed west and caught sight of an enormous land mass."[72]

It would be another eighty-six years before the Vikings would try to settle this unknown land. Historians are not sure why it took so long for the Vikings to do so, but some suspect that a famine in Iceland around the 980s might have forced some to think of moving to a new place. Historian Magnusson reinforces this idea, saying, "It was not until 978, two years after Iceland had suffered a grievous famine in 976, that a party of prospective settlers from the stricken western districts tried to establish a colony on Greenland."[73]

The first wave of colonists encountered a very harsh winter, and returned to Iceland. Three years later, however, another Viking attempted to colonize Greenland. His name was Eirik (Erik) the Red. After being banished from Iceland for three years for killing several people, he set sail for Greenland and spent those years exploring and looking for good lands on which to settle. When Eirik returned to Iceland, he thrilled other Vikings with tales of the fertile lands that could be found in Greenland. Although some accounts say that

EIRIK THE RED

One of the best-known Vikings was a loud, violent warrior named Eirik the Red. Two Icelandic sagas, *Graenlendinga saga* (the Greenlanders' Saga) and *Eiriks saga rauda* (Eirik the Red's Saga) recount Eirik's story, which is one of the most famous Viking tales of adventure. Eirik's greatest accomplishment was discovering Greenland, a country that became one of the most prosperous Viking colonies during the Viking Age.

Eirik the Red appears to have come from a family of quick-tempered, violent men. It is unclear when he was born, but historians know that his family originated in Norway. In about 960, his father, Thorvald, was involved in some killings, and Eirik and his father went to Iceland either to escape punishment or because they were banished from Norway.

Iceland had been colonized many years before, so by the time they arrived, the land had been settled, and no good land was left to claim. Eirik managed to find a woman who had a lot of good land, so he married well and settled down to farm. But the peace would not last for long, as historian Magnus Magnusson relates in his book, *Vikings!*

"[Eirik's] slave accidently started a landslide that destroyed a neighbor's home, indignation flared into all-out feuding, and after some bloodshed, Eirik was thrown out of Haukadalur [the settlement where he lived]. He made himself a new base on some islands, but in no time he was embroiled in another bloody feud with a wealthy farmer over the loan of some household fittings. . . . When Eirik came and took them back by force, there was a pitched battle in which several men were killed, including two of the farmer's sons."

The local court banished Eirik for three years, and told him that, if he returned, the family of the dead men could execute him. Soon, Eirik was on a ship sailing far away from Iceland. He took the opportunity to investigate some rumors of a new land that had been sighted to the west. He finally found it and realized that he could become rich and famous as the land's first settler. This distinction would show that he was fearless in adventure, and it would also give him the chance to claim as much fertile land as he wanted—a sure way to achieve lasting wealth. When his three years of banishment were up, he rushed back to Iceland and began to plan a colonizing expedition to Greenland.

Eirik named the new land Greenland to make it sound more attractive to the colonists, most Vikings needed no extra incentives to go. The idea of a new, green country was very appealing to people who had to squeeze a living from poor land year after year, and who had just lived through famine.

Many colonists left for Greenland, and the group split up when they arrived. Eirik the Red took most of them and settled in an area known as Julianehaab, where they established the Eastern Settlement. The rest of the Vikings chose to travel up the coast and settle in the Godthaab area, known as the Western Settlement. For the next few years, wave after wave of Vikings came to Greenland until all the livable land was taken.

Archaeologists have discovered more than three hundred separate farms in the two set-tlements, suggesting that as many as three thousand Vikings lived in Greenland at its peak. This evidence shows that the Vikings who settled in Greenland raised cattle and sheep. They also hunted and fished, which provided much of their food. According to one thirteenth-century account,

> The people of Greenland are few in number, since only part of the land is free enough from ice for human habitation. . . . One learns that the pasturage [land that can be used for pastures] there is good and that the farms are large and prosperous. The farmers are engaged in raising large numbers of cattle and sheep and in making a great deal of butter and cheese; the people live principally on these products and on beef. In addition, they eat meat from reindeer, whales, seals, and bears.[74]

Demise of the Greenland Settlement

The Vikings of Iceland remained there permanently, and most of the people who live in that country today are descended from the Vikings who first made their homes there. The colony on Greenland, on the other hand, did not enjoy such a long existence. By the year 1500, the Greenland settlement was no more. Historians are not sure why the Vikings eventually abandoned Greenland, and no official records or stories exist to shed light on the mystery.

Some theories suggest that a gradual climate change finally destroyed the Vikings' Greenland settlements. During the eleventh and twelfth centuries, the Earth's northern

After being banished from Iceland for killing several people, Eirik the Red (left) sailed for Greenland.

Historians feel that the Vikings abandoned Greenland when icebergs began appearing in sailing lanes near the settlements.

hemisphere was hit with a mini–ice age. As a result, the warm waters around Greenland that were once easy for Viking ships to navigate slowly filled with dangerous ice. Large sheets of floating ice, called ice floes, began appearing in the sailing lanes near the settlements. The cold seasons grew longer, and eventually the Vikings noticed icebergs off the Greenland coast. One medieval account of the history of Greenland described this situation, "When one has sailed over the deepest part of the ocean, he will meet almost at once huge masses of ice in the sea, a phenomenon without parallel anywhere else. . . .There is also ice of a much different shape, the people of Greenland call them icebergs.

They look like mountains rising high out of the sea."[75]

Although scattered contemporary accounts describe some Vikings still in Greenland until the late 1400s, the settlements were slowly dying. In 1492, Pope Alexander VI described the last remnants of the Viking colony, which had by then become Christian:

> The diocese of Gardar [a Catholic area] lies at the bounds of the earth in the land called Greenland. The people there have no bread, wine, or oil; they sustain themselves on dried fish and milk. Very few sailings to Greenland have been possible because of the ice

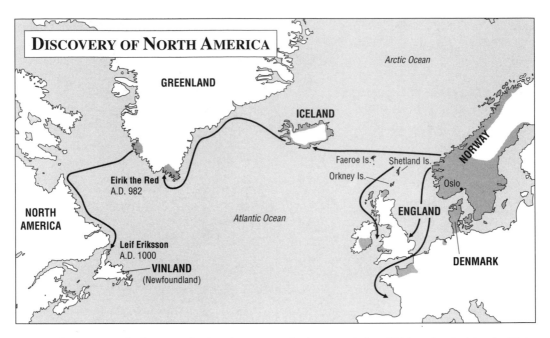

DISCOVERY OF NORTH AMERICA

Arctic Ocean

GREENLAND

ICELAND

NORWAY

Faeroe Is.

Shetland Is.

Orkney Is.

Oslo

Eirik the Red
A.D. 982

NORTH
AMERICA

Atlantic Ocean

ENGLAND

Leif Eriksson
A.D. 1000

VINLAND
(Newfoundland)

DENMARK

in the seas and these only in the month of August, when the ice has melted.[76]

Vikings in North America

Researchers know for certian that the Vikings settled in Iceland and Greenland. One of the most controversial historical questions, however, has been whether or not they were the first Europeans to arrive in North America. Viking sagas contain many references to a green and fruitful land called Vinland, which until recently had been a mystery. Few historians believed that the sagas described an actual place. In the last few decades, however, scholars have concluded that Vinland was in fact North America.

In the 1960s, archaeologists discovered the remains of a Viking settlement and a number of objects in an area of Canada called L'Anse aux Meadows. At the time of the discovery, many historians remained skeptical that the finds proved that Vikings landed in the New World four hundred years before Columbus. However, after exhaustive study of the artifacts, historians realized that the objects could have been made by no other culture except the Vikings. Based on those conclusions, and also on the descriptions of Vinland in the sagas, historians generally accept that the Vikings were indeed the first Europeans in North America.

One Viking story called the *Greenlanders' Saga* tells the story of the first Vikings to see North America. Although the saga does not reveal an exact date, it does relate the story of Bjarni Herjolfssen, who was on his way from Iceland to Greenland when he was blown off course in a storm: "The fair wind failed and northerly gales and fog set in, and for many days [Herjolfssen and his crew] had no idea what their course was. After that they saw the sun again and were able to get their bearings, they hoisted sail, and after a day's sailing they sighted land."[77]

Herjolfssen did not stop to explore the strange land. Instead, he turned around and headed back to Greenland. However, he must have told many people his strange tale, because the *Greenlanders' Saga* also says, "People thought he had shown a great lack of curiosity, and he was criticized for this."[78]

A few years later, around the year 1000, Eirik the Red's son Leif decided to find out whether this land really existed. He bought Herjolfssen's ship, perhaps hoping that the ship might find its way back to the land, and he and a Viking crew retraced Bjarni Herjolfssen's route. After a hard journey, according to another saga, "Leif . . . finally came upon lands whose existence he had never suspected. There were fields of wild wheat growing there, and vines, and among the trees there were maples."[79]

Leif and his crew spent the winter in this new land, which they called Vinland for the vines of grapes they found there. In the spring they filled their boat with timber, grapes, and other goods and set sail back to Greenland. When he returned, his trip successful, Leif became known as Leif the Lucky.

Settling Vinland

Leif never returned to Vinland, but his brothers did. The next year, in 1001, Leif's brother Thorvald borrowed Leif's boat and sailed to Vinland, where he and his crew spent the winter in the huts that Leif's expedition had built the winter before. These Vikings explored the areas around their camp, fishing for salmon in the rivers and sailing up and down the coast in good weather. They came in contact with natives whom they called *skraelings*, who wore skins and used boats made of animal skins. Historians believe that these people were the

ancestors of Native American Eskimo tribes who may have lived in the area at the time.

When news of Thorvald's journey reached Greenland and Iceland around 998, other Vikings came to Vinland. One of them, Thorfinn Karlsefni, was a prosperous Viking merchant. His wife, Gudrid, was Eirik the Red's widowed daughter-in-law. They traveled to Vinland with sixty men and five women and a number of cattle, with the hopes of establishing a permanent settlement in the new lands. They occupied the huts that Leif had built and tried to carve out a life. While they were there, Gudrid gave birth to a son, named Snorri Thorfinnsson, who was the first white European ever born in North America.

Abandoning Vinland

The settlement in Vinland eventually failed, however, and all the evidence points to the same reason. The *skraelings*, who had been friendly at first, became increasingly hostile to the tiny Viking outpost. Fighting broke out between the natives and the Vikings, and Thorfinn eventually realized that his small Viking settlement was greatly outnumbered. Although their iron weapons were superior to the weapons of the *skraelings*, the Vikings could not hope to defend themselves against the numbers of warriors fighting against them. So, in about 1002, they packed up what belongings they could carry and sailed away. No other European would see the shores of the New World for another 400 years. Even though the Vinland colony did not survive, it (and ones like it in Greenland, Iceland, and Russia) was an example of the Vikings' spirit of adventure, their courage, and their willingness to explore the unknown in their quest for land, wealth, and honor.

CHAPTER SEVEN

DOWNFALL OF THE VIKING CIVILIZATION

For more than three hundred years, the Vikings explored, traded, attacked, and settled lands throughout the world. In places like England, they commanded power in half of the country. Their influence was so strong in France that an entire region, Normandy, was named for the Northmen (Vikings) who lived there. Their longports and military outposts in Ireland became vibrant towns, that country's first true urban areas. They traded rich goods with the greatest powers in the world and established thriving colonies in Iceland and Greenland, where their beliefs and traditions lived for centuries.

Their power was great, but it was brief. By A.D. 1066, a variety of forces had managed to drive the Vikings back within their own borders of Scandinavia. Their influence in the world grew weak, then disappeared all together. By 1100, the glorious days of the Viking Age were all but forgotten.

The Effect of Christianity

All of these changes came about slowly. At the beginning of the Viking Age, Europe and Great Britain were Christian areas. Hundreds of years before the first Viking fleets plundered Christian monasteries in England and Ireland, the people in those areas had embraced Christian beliefs, and by 793, all of Europe was Christian.

When the Viking invaders encountered Christians, they did not try to obliterate the belief system. Instead, they married local women who were Christian and began to be influenced by those beliefs. Some even mixed the Viking and Christian religions. One ancient document describes a Viking named Helgi the Skinny, who was "very mixed up in his faith; he believed in Christ, but prayed to Thor on sea-journeys and in tough situations."[80]

Historians suspect that a great many Vikings shared Helgi's initial confusion. They continued to practice their own religion but also began to add Christian elements. Many Vikings referred to Jesus Christ as the White Christ, and simply added him to the family of gods they already worshipped. Historian Roesdahl says, "Throughout the Viking Age there were Scandinavians who professed the Christian faith sincerely, and others who had included Christ in the large pantheon of Scandinavian gods, and even made sacrifices to him on certain occasions."[81]

A Viking settlement lies in ruins somewhere in Greenland. By 1100, the Viking Age had come to a close.

The Missionaries

The Vikings who returned home from raids and settlements in England, Ireland, and France also brought Christian beliefs with them. Historians are not clear as to how many of these Christian converts returned to spread the word, but they are certain that many Vikings were familiar with Christianity when the first Christian missionaries arrived in Scandinavia during the eighth century.

The earliest documented account of a missionary in Viking lands was a monk known as Willibrod, who, during the eighth century, tried unsuccessfully to convert the Danish Vikings. About one hundred years later, another Christian named Ebo, archbishop of Reims (an area of France) baptized many peo-

ple in Denmark. From that time on, a number of Christians traveled to Scandinavia to convert the Vikings, whom they called heathens, to the ways of Christ.

These missionaries were smart in their efforts at winning converts. Many of them were very familiar with the beliefs and traditions of the Vikings, and they used this knowledge to introduce Christianity to the culture. The missionaries understood the value that the people placed on honor and loyalty. They set out to impress the leaders with great shows of respect. Realizing that the Vikings valued honesty, the missionaries strove to show them that they were honorable in their own Christian beliefs. Historian Roesdahl describes this,

> [The missionaries] normally sought permission from the king or local lord

and it is mentioned several times that they brought them rich gifts and held great feasts. They were treated as guests and were given a form of guest protection. Christian documents praised missionaries for their sincere preaching of the Gospel, their piety, learning, good sense in daily life, chastity and good deeds. That they lived according to their teaching impressed the pagans.[82]

Missionaries also understood that the Viking people believed in loyalty to a respected leader, and that they would follow that leader. As a result, Christians focused on converting important and respected members of the Viking aristocracy such as the jarls and the nobles. As they expected, when Viking leaders embraced Christianity, so did their families and followers.

Christian missionaries focused on converting members of the Viking aristocracy such as the jarls and nobles, knowing that others would follow their example.

Why Did the Vikings Agree?

But Christianity was more than just a religious belief. For the pragmatic Vikings, converting made good economic and political sense. For example, many foreign kings were Christian, and they were much more willing to help a Viking leader who also believed—or said he did. There are many instances of Vikings embracing Christianity as a political move, only to revert later. Ordinary Viking warriors in foreign lands also saw the sense in converting, because new converts usually received clothing and gifts. Roesdahl explains, "Many Vikings were baptized abroad, some of them several times, for . . . the ceremony meant new clothes, a baptismal gift and a baptismal feast."[83]

Furthermore, many Viking leaders who traveled abroad saw how powerful and rich the Christian church was in other lands. The church provided money and support during war in some cases and also had the power to convince local populations to support (or ignore) a king. Religious officials like bishops and monks influenced English and French leaders as well. Seeing this, the Vikings quickly understood that it would be advantageous to have the Christian church on their side, and they began converting.

Christianity also had an impact on the Vikings' trade relationships. Many important traders would not do business with so-called heathen Vikings, nor bring their goods to non-Christian Viking towns. As a result, Viking leaders who controlled important trading cities such as Birka and Hedeby in Scandinavia allowed missionaries to build churches and convert the local populations as a way to encourage good trade relations. Although there were usually stipulations that the people could worship the old gods as well as the new, many Vikings slowly adopted the new faith.

By the end of the Viking Age, most of Scandinavia had converted to Christianity. The people who lived in Iceland also voted to accept Christianity as part of their religion; in Greenland, Leif the Lucky, who had converted to Christianity while on a visit to Norway, brought a priest back with him. Slowly, the priest also converted most of the Greenlanders to the new faith.

Effects of Christianity on the Viking Culture

Christianity eliminated many of the old customs and traditions that made the Viking way of life unique. The church forbade many of the customs that the Vikings took for granted, such as plunder and attack to gain wealth. And it outlawed slavery, a major part of the

Viking economy. Slowly the slave trade was eliminated, and the money that came with it disappeared.

Furthermore, the missionaries condemned powerful gods, who were a living, real part of Viking daily life. In an attempt to show that Christ was more powerful than the Viking gods, Christian missionaries and members of the clergy purposefully destroyed pagan sanctuaries and objects. When the Christians were not punished by the gods for those acts, the Vikings saw it as a sign that what the Christians said was true—the one God was indeed more powerful than their deities. As a result, the daily rituals and prayers that were a vital part of the Viking civilization gradually died out.

The Last Battles

By the beginning of the eleventh century, the Viking civilization had peaked. All of the available land in Scandinavia had long since been claimed, and the new lands of Iceland and Greenland were full. The days of English, French, and Irish conquest and settlement had long since passed, and most of the Vikings who lived in those areas had fully assimilated into the local cultures. Their children spoke other languages and followed other customs.

In Scandinavia, the old system of local jarls and chieftains controlling large estates was gradually being replaced by powerful kings who commanded large areas. Denmark, Sweden, and Norway had become separate kingdoms, although the Vikings who lived there spoke the same language and continued to hold similar beliefs.

However, a few strong, adventurous Vikings still thirsted for power and glory. In the late 900s, these men began raiding along

STAVE CHURCHES

One of the most unique and lasting artifacts from the late years of the Viking Age are the structures known as stave churches, some of which still exist in Scandinavia. They are beautiful examples of Viking architecture.

Stave churches were small, wooden buildings that were a series of rectangular walls built on top of one another to form a boxy structure. The roofs were adorned with animal head carvings and other decorations. Inside, although the buildings are clearly made for Christian worship, the walls and doorways were covered with elaborate carvings of twisting vines and animals. These carvings do not specifically depict any pagan beliefs, but their wild and untamed images give the feelings of the restless spirit of the Vikings of the past.

Despite their unique carvings and designs, stave churches were made for Christian worship.

the English coastline again. Although it had been years since Vikings had attacked English and Irish towns, this latest threat lasted for more than a decade, defeating English armies and wreaking havoc in the countryside.

The new Viking armies were led by two powerful men: a Norwegian warrior named Olaf Tryggvason and the king of Denmark, Svein Forkbeard. After many successful raids, including an assault against the city of Lon-

don, the two men returned to Scandinavia. Historian Brondsted describes these events, saying,

When [Olaf] arrived on the Thames [River in England] in 994 he was accompanied by the Danish king, Svein Forkbeard. With a joint fleet of about a hundred long ships, and presumably at least two thousand men, they attacked London; but the city beat off the assault, and the Vikings had to be content with plundering southeast England and finally accepting sixteen thousand pounds of silver to leave.[84]

Cnut Comes to Power

Vikings continued to raid England off and on for the next ten years. However, in 1013 Forkbeard decided he wanted to be king of England as well as Denmark, so he launched a massive attack. His army swept through England, eventually defeating the entire country. Forkbeard, a Viking, then declared himself king of England.

It was not to last, however. He died a few months later, leaving his teenage son Cnut to succeed him. After years of fierce warfare against Viking foes who wanted to control England, Cnut finally established his own claim to the English throne, as well as the thrones of Denmark and Norway.

Thus, he became one of the most powerful Vikings in the world. Cnut was loved by his English subjects. He kept other Vikings from attacking England, respected English laws, and supported the Christian church. Under his rule, England once again became strong and stable.

When Cnut died in 1035, the stability shattered. He had no children, so others quickly stepped in to claim the throne. His stepson Edward eventually became king of England. In Norway, Harald Sigurdsson became king.

During this time, far away in the Normandy area of France, a young man named William was born. The descendant of a famous Viking warrior named Rollo, he would eventually play a major role in the destruction of the Viking civilization.

1066: The Defeat of the Vikings

In January 1066, King Edward of England died. His brother-in-law, Harald Godwinsson, also a Viking, assumed the throne in England. Harald Sigurdsson, king of Norway, was not content with being just king of Norway. He wanted the English crown as well.

Harald Sigurdsson, who was also called Harald Hardrade, which means hard ruler, was the last of the great Viking sea-kings. He was large, loud, adventurous, and in all respects a true Viking warrior. One Viking saga called *King Harald's Saga* described him:

Upon the death of Edward in 1066, William of Normandy sought to obtain control of England.

93

TH E   V I K I N G S

King Harald surpassed all other men in shrewdness and resourcefulness. He was an outstandingly brave warrior, and he also had great victory luck. He was brutal to his enemies, and dealt ruthlessly with any opposition. He was exceptionally greedy for power and wealth; but he was very generous to those of his friends who were dear to him. . . . He was a handsome man of great presence. He was fair-haired, with a fair beard and long moustaches. One of his eyebrows was set slightly higher than the other. He had large, well-shaped hands and feet. He was five ells tall [well over six feet].[85]

Harald Sigurdsson gathered thousands of Viking warriors and sailed to England, convinced that he could defeat the weaker Harald Godwinsson. At the same time, news of Edward's death reached William in Normandy. William had spent many years with Edward in England, and he later claimed that Edward had promised him the English throne. So William began amassing his own army to ensure Edward would make good on that promise.

Three men, all of strong Viking blood, now vied for the powerful throne of England. In September, Harald Sigurdsson landed in England and immediately his huge Viking force began smashing through the countryside. He fought small English forces but easily defeated them and took the city of York. Sigurdsson was confident that the king's army would be defeated as easily.

Attack at Stamford Bridge

He was completely unprepared when King Harald Godwinsson's English army attacked without warning on September 25, 1066, at Stamford Bridge, a few miles east of York. According to legend, the battle was hard and furious, filled with heroic deeds and astounding bravery. One account describes a Viking warrior in Harald Sigurdsson's army saying, "A giant Norwegian defended the bridge . . . to give his comrades time to muster [come together]; he killed countless assailants with his battle-axe before someone crept underneath the bridge and killed him with an upward jab through a gap in the timbers."[86]

The battle raged all afternoon. No one knew who would be victorious, for both sides fought fiercely. Finally, at the height of the battle, says King Harald's Saga,

> [Harald Sigurdsson] fell into such a fury of battle that he rushed forward ahead of his troops, hewing [striking] with both hands. Neither helmet nor armor could withstand him, and everyone in his path gave way before him. It looked then as if the English were on the point of being routed. . . . But now King Harald Sigurdsson was struck in the throat by an arrow, and that was his death-wound.[87]

The Battle of Hastings

King Harald of England allowed the defeated Vikings to leave safely, and the few who were left limped back to Norway. But Godwinsson was still in danger. Two days after the battle of Stamford Bridge, William of Normandy set sail for England. Godwinsson rushed his troops to Hastings, an area near the southern coast of England, where they met the Norman army.

The Battle of Hastings is considered to be one of the most important battles ever fought

Despite his victory over Harald Sigurdsson at the Battle of Stamford Bridge, King Harald Godwinsson eventually lost control of England to William of Normandy.

in world history because the winner of that one battle would become one of the world's most powerful leaders. For a time that day, it seemed as if the Vikings who ruled England would be victorious. The Viking civilization had a chance to live on for centuries.

But it was not to be. After a day of fierce battle, King Harald Godwinsson, Viking king of England, was killed, and his death ended the Battle of Hastings. William of Normandy declared victory.

On Christmas day 1066, William was crowned king of England, and with him came a completely new way of life. Although William was a Viking by descent, he was thoroughly French. Like many Vikings in Normandy before him, William had been completely assimilated into the French cul-

ture, leaving his Viking past behind. When he became king of England, he brought the French culture, government, and language to his new country. Norman nobles seized control of many parts of England. The Vikings who lived in the Danelaw, the area of England controlled by the Vikings, and in other parts of England gradually fell under the influence of this new government, and assimilated over time into the new culture that William introduced to England. The great Viking Age was over.

After the Battle

The changes came slowly. For most Vikings, life continued as it had for centuries. Farmers still tended their livestock; traders continued to buy and sell; and Viking adventurers still set

THE BAYEUX TAPESTRY

One of the most remarkable historical documents to survive from the Viking Age is not a book; it is a large embroidery that tells the story of the Battle of Hastings (1066) in pictures. Called the Bayeux Tapestry, this embroidery is a strip of linen more than two hundred feet long and about two feet wide. Historians are uncertain about exactly who commissioned the work, but some speculate that William of Normandy's half-brother, Bishop Odo of Bayeux, commanded that the tapestry be made to commemorate William's victory in England.

The Bayeux Tapestry shows the events that led up to William's invasion of England and his victory at the Battle of Hastings. Because it was made by the victors, some historians suspect that the events depicted on the tapestry have been embellished somewhat. But it is one of the most complete accounts of the Battle of Hastings, and other scholars look to it for clues about the events that led up to the famous battle and what happened during the battle itself.

The true treasure of the tapestry is that it shows the clothing, hairstyles, ships, and other elements of daily life that were common in 1066. No other original artifact or document from the time is so detailed and complete.

No one knows what purpose Bishop Odo had in mind when he asked that the embroidery be made. Some speculate that it was to be part of William's coronation. Others suggest that it was made for the bishop's new cathedral, which was under construction. Regardless, it remains one of the greatest lasting documents of a Viking Age battle.

The Bayeux Tapestry provides a detailed and accurate record of the Battle of Hastings.

out to raid and plunder, although this was becoming more rare. During the twelfth and thirteenth centuries, Denmark and Sweden expanded into areas around the Baltic and into Finland. They sent soldiers on the Crusades, a series of Christian battles in the Holy Land against the Muslims. But there would be no more great Viking migrations, no terrifying Viking raids, and no exciting Viking explorations and adventures to faraway, unknown places.

In Iceland, however, the Viking culture thrived. Because this settlement was so isolated from the rest of the world, the people were unaffected by the defeat of the Vikings at Hastings and the subsequent decline of the Viking culture. The Icelandic people held on to the Viking ways of life for many generations. It was there that the stories of the Viking gods and the great sagas about past adventures survived. And it was in Iceland that one of the greatest Viking writers and historians, Snorri Sturluson, lived. He recorded much of the Viking culture and mythology that would otherwise have been lost.

Snorri Sturluson

Sturluson was born in Iceland in 1179. As a young boy, he was captivated by the old stories the elders told. As he grew, Sturluson acquired a great deal of knowledge of Viking myth and legend, as well as respect for the old ways. He was dismayed at the fact that the old stories and customs were dying away. As an adult in the early 1200s, Sturluson wrote two volumes that recorded both the history and the myth of the Vikings, the *Prose Edda* and the *Heimskringla*.

The *Prose Edda* is a poetry handbook. In this work, Sturluson recounted the legends of mythology in an entertaining way. He also gave detailed instructions on how the poetry was composed. His *Heimskringla* is a history of the Norwegian kings from their legendary beginnings as descendants of the god Odin. Scholars believe that Sturluson based the *Heimskringla* on earlier histories, but he gathered a great deal of new material on his own, including facts and stories from the poetry and legends he had heard so often as a child.

Because Sturluson mixed fantasy, myth, and poetry with historical events, historians dismiss much of his writing as fiction. However, they believe that Sturluson's descriptions of some aspects of Viking life are accurate, and they study the texts to glean information about the early Viking culture. Today, these works are considered to be some of the most influential and lasting records of what the Viking culture might have been like.

Lasting Effects

Regardless of these efforts, the Viking culture did indeed fade away. The Vikings had so successfully assimilated into the cultures they came into contact with that their original culture was lost. For centuries after the great Viking Age, the Vikings were remembered as ghosts from the past, and their reputation as bloodthirsty pagan warriors lingered on. Although Scandinavia continued to thrive and grow, it was no longer a powerful land filled with adventurous Vikings willing to risk their lives to explore new lands. The descendants of the Viking settlers in England, France, and Russia gradually forgot their roots in Viking culture and became English, French, and Russian.

The Viking civilization, however, continued to influence the world in small ways. For example, many Viking place-names continued to be used in areas where Vikings had settled.

Pictured is a replica of a Viking long ship. As they recreate their ships and voyages, archaeologists and historians are continually amazed by the Vikings' accomplishments.

In English, some days of the week were named for Viking gods, such as Wednesday for Odin's Day, Thursday for Thor's Day and Friday for Frey's Day.

The Vikings' ideas about law continued to influence governments throughout the Western world. Their system of allotting land to trusted members of a leader's army was the foundation for the feudal system, a governmental philosophy that was in place in Europe for more than four hundred years after the Viking Age. And the Viking idea of allowing ordinary citizens to have a say in government, developed in the Viking civilization as the Thing, was the basis of many democracies and republics founded in later centuries. Some historians suspect that the Founding Fathers of the United States may have looked to the ancient Viking Things for ideas on how to develop their new governmental system.

Their shipbuilding innovations influenced future navigation, and many of their inventions were copied and improved upon. Archaeologists and historians continue to marvel at the Vikings' amazing long ships. Some even recreate Viking ships and set out on voyages of their own to experience what it must have been like for the Vikings to explore the world and to see whether the Vikings' ships could have actually made the long voyages recorded in the sagas.

But the most lasting legacy of the Vikings was their reputation as fearless, adventuresome spirits who met life and death with humor, strength, and bravery. This image of the Viking, a free spirit facing the sea and the wind with wide eyes and a devilish grin, continues to linger in movies, music, and literature throughout the world. It is this spirit of freedom and independence that gave the Vikings such power during their golden Viking Age, and it is also what keeps their memory alive today.

NOTES

Chapter 1: Before the Viking Age

1. James Graham-Campbell and Dafydd Kidd, *The Vikings*. London: British Museum Publications, 1980, p. 20.
2. F. Donald Logan, *The Vikings in History*. London: Routledge, 1983, p. 17.
3. Logan, *The Vikings in History*, p. 19.
4. Graham-Campbell and Kidd, *Vikings*, p. 17.
5. Else Roesdahl, *The Vikings*. London: Penguin Books, 1987, p. 28.
6. Colleen Batey, Helen Clarke, R. I. Page, and Neil S. Price, *Cultural Atlas of the Viking World*. New York: Facts on File, 1994, p. 23.
7. Batey, Clarke, Page, and Price, *Cultural Atlas*, p. 27.
8. Graham-Campbell and Kidd, *Vikings*, p. 21.
9. P. H. Sawyer, *Kings and Vikings: Scandinavia and Europe* A.D. *700–1100*. London: Methuen & Co., 1982, p. 65.
10. Edvard Henriksen, *Scandinavia Past and Present*. Odense, Denmark: Arnkrone, 1959, p. 65.

Chapter 2: Raids and Warfare

11. Quoted in Roesdahl, *Vikings*, p. 196.
12. Quoted in Roesdahl, *Vikings*, p. 188.
13. Quoted in Roesdahl, *Vikings*, p. 188.

14. Quoted in Magnus Magnusson, *Vikings!* New York: E. P. Dutton, 1980, p. 31.
15. Quoted in Magnusson, *Vikings!*, p. 32.
16. Quoted in David M. Wilson, *The Vikings and Their Origins*. London: Thames and Hudson, 1970, p. 72.
17. Roesdahl, *Vikings*, p. 223.
18. Roesdahl, *Vikings*, p. 223.
19. Johannes Brondsted, *The Vikings*. London: Penguin Books, 1960, p. 139.
20. Graham-Campbell and Kidd, *Vikings*, p. 25.
21. Roesdahl, *Vikings*, p. 83.
22. Quoted in Jacqueline Simpson, *Everyday Life in the Viking Age*. London: B. T. Batsford Ltd., 1967, p. 120.
23. Roesdahl, *Vikings*, p. 143.

Chapter 3: Settling Down

24. Batey, Clarke, Page, and Price, *Cultural Atlas*, p. 125.
25. Batey, Clarke, Page, and Price, *Cultural Atlas*, p. 125.
26. Magnusson, *Vikings!*, p. 127.
27. Quoted in Batey, Clarke, Page, and Price, *Cultural Atlas*, p. 125.
28. Quoted in Sawyer, *Kings and Vikings*, p. 84.
29. Quoted in Logan, *The Vikings in History*, p. 129.

30. Logan, *The Vikings in History*, p. 167.

31. Quoted in Logan, *The Vikings in History*, p. 165.

32. Judith Jesch, *Women in the Viking Age*. Woodbridge, England: Boydell Press, 1991, p. 40.

33. Roesdahl, *Vikings*, p. 117.

34. Gwyn Jones, *A History of the Vikings*. Oxford, England: Oxford University Press, 1984, p. 157.

35. Batey, Clarke, Page, and Price, *Cultural Atlas*, p. 81.

36. Quoted in Roesdahl, *Vikings*, p. 118.

Chapter 4: Viking Society

37. Jones, *History of the Vikings*, p. 151.

38. Roesdahl, *Vikings*, p. 64.

39. Jones, *History of the Vikings*, p. 151.

40. Quoted in Jones, *History of the Vikings*, p. 152.

41. Quoted in Roesdahl, *Vikings*, p. 72.

42. Jones, *History of the Vikings*, p. 155.

43. Wilson, *The Vikings and Their Origins*, p. 114.

44. Jones, *History of the Vikings*, p. 148.

45. Quoted in Simpson, *Everyday Life in the Viking Age*, p. 58.

Chapter 5: Religion and Spiritual Beliefs

46. Henricksen, *Scandinavia Past and Present*, p. 130.

47. Henricksen, *Scandinavia Past and Present*, pp. 131–32.

48. Kevin Crossley-Holland, *The Norse Myths*. New York: Pantheon Books,

1980, p. xix.

49. Quoted in Crossley-Holland, *Norse Myths*, p. xxv.

50. Ingri D'Aulaire and Edgar Darin D'Aulaire, *Norse Gods and Giants*. New York, Doubleday & Co., 1967, p. 38.

51. Brondsted, *Vikings*, p. 274.

52. Crossley-Holland, *Norse Myths*, p. xxvi.

53. Crossley-Holland, *Norse Myths*, p. xxvi.

54. Quoted in Crossley-Holland, *Norse Myths*, p. xxvii.

55. Quoted in Crossley-Holland, *Norse Myths*, p. xxix.

56. Brondsted, *Vikings*, p. 281.

57. Brondsted, *Vikings*, p. 289.

58. Brondsted, *Vikings*, p. 291.

59. Quoted in Simpson, *Everyday Life in the Viking Age*, p. 191.

60. Simpson, *Everyday Life in the Viking Age*, p. 192.

61. Quoted in Simpson, *Everyday Life in the Viking Age*, p. 193.

Chapter 6: The Golden Age of Viking Exploration

62. Brondsted, *Vikings*, p. 263.

63. Roesdahl, *Vikings*, p. 277.

64. Quoted in Magnusson, *Vikings!*, pp. 110–11.

65. Quoted in Magnusson, *Vikings!*, pp. 116–17.

66. Magnusson, *Vikings!*, p. 120.

67. Logan, *Vikings in History*, p. 61.

68. Quoted in Logan, *Vikings in History*, p. 63.

69. Quoted in Logan, *Vikings in History*, p. 63.

70. Quoted in Logan, *Vikings in History*, p. 63.

71. Roesdahl, *Vikings*, p. 263.

72. Quoted in Logan, *Vikings in History*, p. 71.

73. Magnusson, *Vikings!*, p. 213.

74. Quoted in Logan, *Vikings in History*, p. 75.

75. Quoted in Logan, *Vikings in History*, p. 78.

76. Quoted in Logan, *Vikings in History*, p. 79.

77. Quoted in Magnusson, *Vikings!*, p. 221.

78. Quoted in Magnusson, *Vikings!*, p. 222.

79. Quoted in Magnusson, *Vikings!*, p. 222.

Chapter 7: Downfall of the Viking Civilization

80. Quoted in Batey, Clarke, Page, and Price, *Cultural Atlas*, p. 115.

81. Roesdahl, *Vikings*, pp. 158–59.

82. Roesdahl, *Vikings*, p. 161.

83. Roesdahl, *Vikings*, p. 158.

84. Brondsted, *Vikings*, p. 78.

85. Quoted in Magnusson, *Vikings!*, p. 284.

86. Quoted in Magnusson, *Vikings!*, p. 310.

87. Quoted in Magnusson, *Vikings!*, p. 310.

FOR FURTHER READING

Ingri D'Aulaire and Edgar Darin D'Aulaire, *Norse Gods and Giants*. New York: Doubleday & Co., 1967, p. 38. This children's book presents the Vikings gods and myths in a lively, easy-to-follow format with lovely illustrations.

Mary J. Dobson, *Vile Vikings (Smelly Old History)*. London: Oxford University Press, 1998. The Smelly Old History series presents historical eras with colorful, cartoon stories and the smells of life from the time.

Susan M. Margeson, *Eyewitness: Vikings*. London, D. K. Publishing, 2000. This book features clear color photos that explain the history and lifestyles of the Vikings in an easy-to-understand format.

Stewart Ross, *Read About Vikings*. New York: Millbrook Press, 2000. This book presents the Vikings in a straightforward, easy-to-read manner.

Rachel Wright, *The Viking News*. New York: Candlewick Press, 1998. This book presents Viking history in a modern newspaper format, complete with ads for common Viking items.

WORKS CONSULTED

Bertil Almgren, *The Viking*. Göteborg, Sweden: A. B. Nordbok, 1995. This easy-to-read history is filled with line drawings that show the daily life of the Vikings.

Holger Arbman, *The Vikings*. New York: Praeger Publishers, 1961. A scholarly work that touches on many aspects of the Viking civilization.

Colleen Batey, Helen Clarke, R. I. Page, and Neil S. Price, *Cultural Atlas of the Viking World*. New York: Facts on File, 1994. An interesting, densely packed compendium of Viking culture and history.

Johannes Brondsted, *The Vikings*. London: Penguin Books, 1960. Brondsted, one of the most respected scholars of Viking civilization, presents his findings in this academic work.

Helen Clarke and Bjorn Ambrosian, *Towns in the Viking Age*. New York: St. Martin's Press, 1991. This work is an academic look at the archaeology and psychology behind the rise of towns during the Viking Age.

Kevin Crossley-Holland, *The Norse Myths*. New York: Pantheon Books, 1980. The author recounts a series of lively Viking myths as well as providing a good explanation of Viking beliefs and mythology.

H. R. Ellis Davidson, *Gods and Myths of Northern Europe*. Harmondsworth, Middlesex, England: Penguin Books, Ltd., 1964. A scholarly work that discusses the origins and structure of the Norse mythology.

Peter G. Foote and David M. Wilson, *The Viking Achievement*. New York: Praeger Publishers, 1970. Two of the foremost experts in Viking history join to write a dense, academic account of the history of the Northmen.

James Graham-Campbell and Dafydd Kidd, *The Vikings*. London: British Museum Publications, 1980. Two eminent historians have compiled a thoughtful, easy-to-understand book on the history of the Vikings.

Edvard Henriksen, *Scandinavia Past and Present*. Odense, Denmark: Arnkrone, 1959. This book, part of a larger series of the history of Scandinavia, is a weighty account of the first few thousand centuries of Scandinavian history from the Ice Age until the Middle Ages.

Judith Jesch, *Women of the Viking Age*. Woodbridge, England: Boydell Press, 1991. Jesch pieces together information from a variety of sources to create a picture of what a Viking woman's life might have been like.

Gwyn Jones, *A History of the Vikings*. Oxford, England: Oxford University Press, 1984. This small volume is filled with historical detail and information that bring the Vikings alive.

F. Donald Logan, *The Vikings in History*. London: Routledge, 1983. Although this is clearly a scholarly work, Logan manages to present it in a manner that is both friendly and easy to digest.

Magnus Magnusson, *Vikings!* New York: E. P. Dutton, 1980. The Scandinavian historian presents a lively account of events and personalities of the Viking Age.

Else Roesdahl, *The Vikings*. London: Penguin Books, 1987. A good overview of Viking history and culture, with many photographs illustrating famous Viking artifacts and locations.

P. H. Sawyer, *The Age of the Vikings*. London: Camelot Press, 1962. A scholarly work that focuses on the Vikings and others who lived during that time in European history.

———, *Kings and Vikings: Scandinavia and Europe* A.D. *700–1100*. London: Methuen & Co., 1982. This work includes information on the Viking system of kingship and nobility as well as facts about the events in the world during the Viking Age.

Jacqueline Simpson, *Everyday Life in the Viking Age*. London: B. T. Batsford Ltd., 1967. A light, easy-to-read book that covers a variety of topics, including Viking dress, clothing, homes, farms, and daily life.

Priit Vesilind, "In Search of the Vikings," *National Geographic*, May 2000. An in-depth article about the history of the Vikings and their travels through the world.

David M. Wilson, *The Vikings and Their Origins*. London: Thames and Hudson, 1970. A small, copiously illustrated overview of Viking history and culture.

INDEX

PICTURE CREDITS

ABOUT THE AUTHOR

Award-winning children's magazine editor and writer Allison Lassieur has published more than two dozen books about history, world cultures, current events, science, and health. She has written for magazines such as *National Geographic World*, *Highlights for Children*, *Scholastic News*, and *Disney Adventures*, and she also writes puzzle books and computer-game materials. In addition to writing, Ms. Lassieur studies medieval textile history. She lives and works with her two cats, Ulysses and Oberon, in a one-hundred-year-old house in Easton, Pennsylvania.